ADVANCE PRAISE

"An insightful look at leadership using principles demonstrated by characters in the *Ted Lasso* show. In Ted-like style, they keep things simple and practical while inserting humor and lots of fun just like each episode!"

—ARLIN SORENSEN, VP Ecosystem Evangelism ConnectWise

"A fun-to-read, easy-to-action book that is rich in principles. If you want one book on leadership, start here!"

—SCOTT LEVY, CEO ResultMaps

"A relatable read, especially for *Ted Lasso* fans, with tangible steps to becoming a better version of yourself and building more functional teams."

—EMILY GLASS, CEO SyncroMSP

"The dynamic duo, Marnie and Nick, scores big-time with a wealth of practical wisdom, just like our favorite coach, Ted Lasso. They've taken the heartwarming lessons from the TV series and crafted them into an MVP of a book on leadership and teamwork!"

—SUNNY KAILA, Author, *Talentpreneurship*

"Much like Ted Lasso's unwavering optimism and genuine empathy, *Lead It Like Lasso* is a beacon of inspiration for anyone looking to lead with heart and drive meaningful changes. It reminds us that success in business is not just about strategy and metrics but also about fostering a culture of kindness, resilience, and unwavering belief in the potential of you and your team."

—KYLE SPOONER, VP MSP Geek

LEAD IT LIKE LASSO

A Leadership Book for Life.
Your Life.

Unofficial, unauthorized, and uncensored

MARNIE STOCKMAN, ED.D. & NICK CONIGLIO

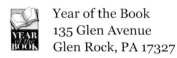
Year of the Book
135 Glen Avenue
Glen Rock, PA 17327

ISBN: 978-1-64649-370-8 (hardcover)
ISBN: 978-1-64649-371-5 (paperback)
ISBN: 978-1-64649-372-2 (e-book)

DEDICATION

To our family and friends,
thanks for being our Diamond Dogs.

To Ted Lasso fans

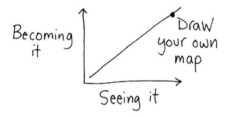

To those who have not (yet) seen *Ted Lasso* – we 'Believe' you will become a fan and get inspired by Ted's leadership lessons. But…

SPOILER ALERT!!! (We really really really recommend you watch the show, as these leadership lessons are applicable to all, but so much funnier for fans 😊)

Finally, a fair warning – We asked imaginary Roy Kent to write the foreword, sooooo yep, cussing ensues. Don't worry, the rest of the book is totally PG.

CONTENTS

FOREWORD

Fuuuuck! No! Just no!

I hate writing. (Have you seen my scribbled note to Keeley?!) No. I didn't want to write the foreword for this book.

But then…

F U C K! I read it. And… now I have to write the fucking foreword for this book.

Why? They fucking surprised me and that's right hard to do. I was minding my own fucking business and I got a postcard. A postcard! What is this 1923?! It gets worse. It was a postcard of Ted Lasso's fucking mustache, and it said, "Roy, I mustache you a question?"

I thought Yankee Doodle himself sent the card. No. Instead it was two fucking nobodies – Marnie Stockman and Nick Coniglio. Who the fuck are they?! And asking me to write a foreword?

I'll tell you who they are. They are Marnie *fucking* Stockman and Nick *fucking* Coniglio, authors of this book *Lead It Like Lasso*. And it is fucking amazing.

I could go on, but writing books is more Trent Crimm's thing. Just sit down, shut up, and read the fucking book! You can thank me later.

Whistle! Whistle!

We wish!

i

PREFACE

In an odd start to this book, we would agree with Roy Kent's first impression of us. We are *nobodies*.

Our spouses, friends, colleagues, and kids (now that they are no longer in high school) might argue that we are *somebodies* to them. But they would agree that in the context of "the whole wide world," we are relative nobodies.

That said, on Halloween 2019, we and two other business partners launched a business called Lifecycle Insights. Lifecycle Insights is a software platform that helps managed service providers (MSPs) grow their businesses. Our goal was to grow the company for 3-5 years then sell for 8 figures.

And right before Season 3 of *Ted Lasso* aired in 2023, we did exactly that.

Some things we would like to point out:

1) Prior to starting the business, we didn't even know what MSPs were.

2) We had never launched a software company before.

3) We had never owned a business before. (Okay, Marnie owned a knitting shop, but that is definitely a story for a different day.)

4) We didn't get outside funding. We bootstrapped the whole thing for a total investment of $16,000. (Heck, Rebecca Welton has that much cash in her purse.)

Like Ted Lasso, we had to learn a new language... even though for both Ted and us, it was still English! We also had to adapt to a completely new environment. We had to figure out the players. We had to build a team, learn new skills, and create a system.

Did we ever ask ourselves the question Ted asked Beard: "Are we crazy for doing this?"

Like Ted, we only asked ourselves that question once. Here's why...

We believed.

We believed we had found a problem we could solve. We believed we could build a company. (Nick had helped grow four companies to acquisition, just never as an owner.) We believed in hard work. Most importantly, we believed in a culture of Raving Fans.

Prior to starting that company, we worked together and got acquired and acquired and acquired again. We have seen the good, the bad, and the ugly of how some businesses are run and how some leaders lead. No one wants to work for the Rupert Mannions of the world!

We wanted to do things differently. We believed we could.

Now, like Ted, we weren't flying completely blind. Marnie has been a teacher, administrator, and customer success executive, and she holds a doctorate in leadership. Nick has run tech development teams, support teams, and has over two decades of experience participating in executive leadership teams.

Like Lasso, we learned how to win by doing the right things for the right reasons.

Without consciously thinking about it, we had already created our own personal operating systems. Together we strategized to build a business operating system. When we watched *Ted Lasso*, not only did we smile, but we recognized lessons we had learned along the way. We noticed the similarities and differences... because in business, like sports, it is *also* about wins and losses. But like Lasso, we learned how to win by doing the right things for the right reasons.

Internet rave reviews confirm that the writers of *Ted Lasso* were inspired and clever. They tied together strategies from improv comedy to self-help to leadership. We laughed as we connected dots from some of our favorite leadership books. "The harder you work, the luckier you get." Ted said it, but he could have referenced any number of quotes from Malcolm Gladwell's *Outliers: The Story of Success.*[1]

> *This isn't just a leadership book for business... it's a leadership book for life.*

All of this is what inspired us to write this book. We believe we translate the personal leadership lessons that Lasso delighted us with on the pitch into lessons for you. This isn't just a leadership book for business. It is a leadership book for life. Your life.

Let us help you build your personal operating system to Lead It Like Lasso.

Leadership is life!

---

[1] In his book, *Outliers,* Gladwell explores the factors that contribute to high levels of success. He argues that it's not just talent or intelligence that leads to exceptional achievement, but also the amount of time and effort one puts into their pursuits. Gladwell introduces the concept of the "10,000-Hour Rule," which suggests that to achieve mastery in any field, it takes roughly 10,000 hours of deliberate practice.

INTRODUCTION

One of us is outgoing, clever, can rhyme her ass off, and doesn't mind breaking into a goofy jig in public.

The other is quiet, humble, smart, and always asks the right questions.

Clearly, we could be talking about Ted Lasso and Coach Beard. But we're not.

We're talking about us, Marnie Stockman and Nick Coniglio, the authors of this book. We would not be so audacious as to say that we're anywhere near as impressive as Lasso and Beard (although Marnie does make a superior chocolate chip "biscuit"). Yet as we launched, scaled, and sold our multimillion-dollar software company in the same three seasons as *Ted Lasso* won the hearts of fans everywhere, we found some similarities. Not just in our personal traits, but also in our approach to leadership.

What we recognized through the television series is that these leadership lessons help every area of life.

> *You don't need to be a CEO to be a leader.*

You don't need to be a CEO to be a leader. Leaders are everywhere. You can lead in a classroom. You can lead a department. You can lead a team. Most importantly, you need to know how to lead yourself. If we learned nothing else in *Ted Lasso*, we really did learn that leadership is life.

ICYMI²: Recap and Spoiler Alert!

Ted Lasso is a heartwarming and comedic TV series that follows the unexpected journey of Ted Lasso (played by Jason Sudeikis), an American college football coach, who is hired to lead a struggling

---

² ICYMI = In case you missed it

1

English soccer team, AFC Richmond. The show begins with the premise of a fish-out-of-water story, as Ted – who has no prior experience in soccer – is brought to the UK under what seems to be dubious circumstances.

As the story unfolds, it becomes evident that Ted's appointment was driven by the club owner, Rebecca Welton (played by Hannah Waddingham), with an ulterior motive – to sabotage the team due to anger at her ex-husband, a former team owner. However, Ted's unconventional and relentlessly positive approach to coaching, along with his genuine kindness and belief in his players, begins to make a profound impact.

Throughout the series, Ted's infectious optimism and emphasis on team dynamics and personal growth foster a transformative change within the team's players and staff. The show delves into the lives of various characters, each struggling with their own challenges... whether it's the star player Roy Kent (Brett Goldstein) facing his own aging, the young kit man Nathan Shelley (Nick Mohammed) battling self-doubt, or Ted himself managing the distance from his family back in the United States.

The series is not just about sports; it's about relationships, personal growth, and the power of positivity. Ted's leadership style – inspired by his own beliefs and the wisdom of his idol, American basketball coach John Wooden – draws people in and gradually turns skeptics into believers. His bond with his assistant coach, Coach Beard (Brendan Hunt), showcases a friendship built on unwavering support and shared values.

As Ted navigates cultural differences, homesickness, and the challenges of coaching a losing team, he faces both professional and personal obstacles. Yet his ability to connect with people on a deeper level, to value character over wins, and to lead with authenticity and empathy, make him a standout character who transcends traditional sports narratives.

Like so many of you, we connected with the lessons of Lasso. We saw some of ourselves, and more importantly, we saw some of what we could become.

We harbor (or harbour, on the UK side of the pond) an affinity for positivity, a penchant for pushing others to be their best, and a keen understanding that leadership isn't a title, it's a way of life.

> *Leadership isn't a title. It's a way of life.*

Our fascination with the wisdom that Ted Lasso imparts isn't just about binge-watching episodes while munching on popcorn (though we mastered that too). No, it's about embracing a leadership philosophy that plays out beyond football pitches. It's about recognizing that every person, whether orchestrating a boardroom meeting, rallying a locker room pep talk, or conducting the family dinner, wields the power of leadership.

As the story of Lasso unfolds, we didn't just scribble notes and nod in agreement with Ted and Beard's antics. We whiteboarded our own personal and business "operating systems" that had gotten us where we were. We even developed a spreadsheet (charts and graphs and everything) outlining the journey of self-reflection and improvement of the characters as they "leveled up" and became a better version of themselves. We aligned what we had learned, in growing ourselves and in growing our business, with the lessons Ted Lasso delivered week after week. And we want to share!

As students in the world of leadership, we connected many of Lasso's lessons with some of our favorite leadership books.

Fair warning: If you keep a "to read" list, you might want to have it handy. We will have no shortage of suggestions throughout the book.

We took all of the lessons we learned from Lasso, from our experiences, from leadership books and experts, and let them steep. (Sorry, Ted... Marnie loves tea!) The results are in the pages ahead. We show you the blueprint for not only leading, but leading with zest and authenticity. We'll teach you how to craft your own "Operating System" – a guidebook for navigating life, making decisions, and inspiring those around you. It's the ultimate playbook for becoming the best version of yourself, whether you're in the corporate arena, the sporting arena, or just trying to herd your family out the door.

We bet you picked up this book because you enjoyed watching *Ted Lasso*. More than that, you loved the way it made you feel. Our goal is to help you learn to lead and live that same way. Just like any good coach, we will dive into The Rules, The Players, The Training (or *Practice,* as some would say), and The Game.

Time out: If by some chance you are reading this book and have NOT watched *Ted Lasso*, we suggest you go watch the first season. It's just 10 quick episodes. We can almost guarantee that those 5 hours (309 minutes actually) will be worth every penny of an Apple TV+ subscription.

THE RULES

Let's face it. If it wasn't for Coach Beard, Ted would not have been successful. Beard was Ted's (and our) guide to the world of European football (and England) and all of their rules – both written and unwritten. Leadership and life have written and unwritten rules as well. We will start our journey in leading like Lasso by looking at The Rules that can serve as guide rails to get us started with becoming the best we can be.

THE PLAYERS

Just as Ted understood that he needed to get to know his players, it is important for you to know yourself as a leader. We have all dreamed of being one of the characters in *Ted Lasso*, so Part Two will have you take a little assessment to see which character's leadership style resonates most with you. We will then take a look at their leadership strengths and areas where some coaching would be helpful.

TRAINING

Once you really understand yourself, and your team, as Ted did, then you can start to focus on how to maximize your strengths and close some of those gaps. You won't have Roy shouting at you from the sideline, but we will certainly outline ways to grow your skills from some of the masters in literature and greatest leaders of our time.

THE GAME

Once you know your players and have done your training, it's time for the game. In our case, this is real life so we're going to help you outline your playbook for life. This will become your operating system, your personal set of directions to discover the current version of yourself, and unearth what the future you can look like. We have activities, reflections, and other insights to help you on the path to becoming the best version of you that you can be.

Play along by bringing paper and pencil,
your favorite electronic note-taking device,
or go all in with a whiteboard.

Social media is full of fans who have outlined the myriad of Easter eggs that the writers of *Ted Lasso* placed in the show to the delight of their fanbase. We aim to do the same by providing trick plays, extra time, and some penalty kicks. (Oh and spoilers... *so many* spoilers.) What would delight us to no end would be for you to engage with us and our activities that can be found on the website:

LeadItLikeLasso.com

This isn't your grandmother's leadership book. Heck, this isn't even Ted Lasso's grandmother's leadership book. Hold tight. We are hoping you came to play. There is no sidelining you in your life! Let's learn to Lead It Like Lasso.

PART ONE

THE RULES

1 THE RULES

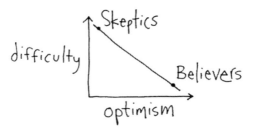

When Ted was hired as the new gaffer (coach) for AFC Richmond, the team, the town, and the entire country made it no secret that they thought he was just a clueless "wanker." But it was clear, even early on, that Ted knew a thing or two about being a good leader...

- From the framed strategic leadership traits of John Wooden's "Pyramid of Success" on his office wall...

- To insisting on "biscuits with the boss" to build trust and a relationship with team-owner Rebecca...

- To eventually getting Roy Kent to understand it "had to be him" who needed to cajole teammates Colin (Billy Harris) and Isaac (Kola Bokinni) to stop bullying Nate the kit man and help build a cohesive locker room.

Ted knew there was "an entire internet" full of written rules about football (aka soccer) that he didn't know. Thankfully for Ted (and American viewers), Coach Beard was there to help impart wisdom about the game. But as Season 1 unfolded, we saw that while Ted might not know the rules of the game, he certainly already had his own leadership operating system and lots of unwritten rules around coaching... and life.

Any coach or leader's operating system refers to the underlying values and strategies that guide their decision-making and actions. It's the fundamental framework and philosophy that shapes how a leader approaches their role – the big idea and strategies about how any organization should operate and succeed.

On the other hand, everyone also has a set of rules that they lead and live by. These could be specific guidelines, organizational policies, and especially personal codes of conduct. "Be curious, not judgmental," was one of Ted's rules. The harmony of one's personal rules with the rules of their broader organization (be it work, team, or community) is what can make or break a culture. As Austrian-American consultant and educator Peter Drucker would say: "Culture eats strategy for breakfast."

One of the most critical strategic elements of any organization is to have a common goal or vision. But if having a common goal would be sufficient to drive success, then just being on a team whose goal is to win a championship should be enough to make it happen. Clearly, it doesn't work that way, even if we ignore the fact that Rebecca was trying to sabotage the whole thing from the get-go.

That is why we want to start with "The Rules."

Don't fret...
There are plenty more elements of leadership
in the Training section. But...

Rules are how we function in our day-to-day lives and in our work. We each have our own personal operating system. For example, "Seize the day... but coffee first" might be one of yours.

Ted figured out early on that the "operating instructions" for Jamie Tartt (played by Phil Dunster) included arrogance, ego, and a fair amount of ball-hogging on the pitch. Ted also knew that if he couldn't get Jamie's personal rules to align with those of the team, then AFC Richmond would never reach any of their goals.

Thanks to a suggestion from Jamie's girlfriend, Keeley (Juno Temple), who said that Jamie responded well to positive reinforcement, Ted spent many an episode working on getting Jamie to change his own rules.

Rules are certainly necessary. They do keep the world, companies, and households from turning into complete chaos. But we are by no means saying that rules are not meant to be broken. What we are saying is that understanding the rules is critical. It is only through *understanding* that we can begin to question those rules, and if necessary, strive to re-write them.

Human history is full of rules being broken – most often replaced with new rules that improve the situation. For instance, consider the monumental achievement of landing on the moon. Back in the 1960s, the established rules of gravity and space exploration seemed insurmountable. Yet, visionaries like NASA's scientists and engineers dared to challenge these norms. They didn't merely accept the limitations imposed by existing rules; they sought to rewrite them. Through innovative thinking, exhaustive research, and unyielding determination, they crafted new paradigms of space travel that eventually led humanity to set foot on a celestial body thousands of miles away.[3]

> *Only through understanding can we begin to question the rules... and if necessary, strive to re-write them.*

Similarly, let's turn our attention to the evolution of basketball. For decades, the sport adhered to a strict two-point scoring system. But visionary thinkers, recognizing the potential to revolutionize the game, dared to question that norm. The introduction of the three-point line was met with skepticism and resistance, yet it ultimately transformed the way the game is played. This seemingly small alteration in the rules unlocked a whole new dimension of strategy, rewarding teams for their prowess in long-range shooting.

---

[3] For the sake of Nate, that's 238,900 miles away. ☺

It is a testament to the power of challenging established norms and seeking to redefine what's possible.

These examples underscore that progress often emerges from the willingness to challenge, and even break, the rules that confine our thinking.

We will share our rules with you along with our leadership principles. We aim to provide you with a basis to understand, hopefully appreciate, adopt, and yes... even question the content in this book. We would be disappointed if you did not connect with us to share personal experiences and thoughts on how we could improve our approach to leadership and your personal rules and operating system.

As Ted said, no topic or question will be "in to touch" (*out of bounds*, as he would say back home). The ultimate goal is for you to create your own definition and rules of leadership to live by.

Many times there are unwritten rules in business. These are often constructed upon the core beliefs of the owners. Before we wrote this book, Nick and Marnie already had established some of those:

◊ Marnie started her adult life as a high school math teacher. In applications, she was always asked her philosophy of education. Her response was:

"I believe it is my responsibility as a teacher and as a human to help each student/person learn and grow to become the best version of themselves."

She still lives by that rule. (Yeah, she's the one like Lasso.)

◊ As a long-suffering Jets fan, Nick has always been fascinated by the relegation/promotion rules of the English Premier League. (Sadly, the J-E-T-S, Jets! Jets! Jets! would no longer be an NFL team if such rules applied.)[4] The writers

---

[4] As a reminder, the EPL has 20 teams. At the end of each season, the bottom 4 teams are relegated to a lower division, and the top 4 teams from

of *Ted Lasso* sucked us in to cheering (often loudly in our own living rooms) for AFC Richmond, hoping to help keep them from relegation. It unified millions of viewers in support of a single rule. Nick's business rule is to unify all of the efforts in a business toward a single goal.

Both of these personal rules played out as we grew our own company:

◊ We started out as a team of co-founders. We each worked to maximize our own potential for the sake of the company. We had to learn all of the elements of running and scaling a software business. We absolutely had to level up as individuals and contributors to the team for the sake of the company.

◊ We set high-level goals from the start and met quarterly, monthly, weekly, and daily to ensure that our actions remained aimed at our target. That focus actually led us to a successful exit and our Rule #2!

But most importantly, through our experiences, our education (both formal and informal), and our gut instincts, we found that we operated on some additional unwritten rules. Don't worry! We decided to write them down to share with you. Of course, we had to start with ...

---

the lower division are promoted to the EPL. Season 1 of *Ted Lasso* culminated with AFC Richmond fighting for their (and their fans') ability to stay in the EPL. The team needed a win against Manchester City to not get relegated. *Spoiler alert: they did not win.*

RULE #1

LEADERSHIP IS LIFE!

The Dani Rojas Rule (named because he's our favorite)

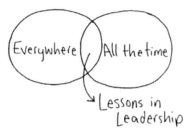

Leadership principles do not just apply to a business setting – they apply to every life setting. Sure, leadership is embodied by a CEO overseeing a company, but leadership is also displayed by a parent raising a child, a camp counselor corralling youth, and a team captain engaging other players. The examples are endless.

When you think about applying Rule #1, you don't have to look far. Think about a store employee leading and training "the new recruit." Of course the lessons would include conversations around the best ways to provide superior customer service. After all, that's this employee's role as a leader at work. But there would also be the opportunity for this trainer to lead in a different way... by sharing some of the "below the line" rules... like tips on how to not get your lunch stolen out of the staff fridge.

Maybe you have created a new rule for yourself and started setting your alarm 15 minutes early in order to fit in some meditation before the mayhem of your day begins. That is just one way you can lead yourself to a better version of you.

Trick Play (i.e., life hack): One key to good leadership is delegation. When Marnie's kids were 16 and 14, she recognized that one of them loved to drive and the other loved to shop. Since Marnie is not a fan of grocery shopping, she started delegating this task to the humans in her house who enjoyed it. That is one of many times she has used leadership principles in her day-to-day life.

RULE #2
DON'T BE A SEAGULL

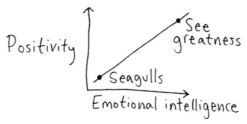

We learned this rule from a business partner. He would say that one mistake he made in a former business was to behave as a "seagull."[5] He said he would swoop in, crap on everything, then leave it for everyone else to clean up. That "crap" would include new ideas that he expected the team to accomplish immediately without regard to their current plan, goals, or objectives.

Being a seagull in business is generally considered detrimental to team morale, productivity, and overall work culture. Effective leadership involves consistent communication, constructive feedback, and active involvement in the development and success of team members. The seagull approach, on the other hand, can have a negative impact in a variety of ways – from being a major distraction to creating a downright toxic work environment.

Being a seagull at home looks a little different. You and your child have discussed the importance of the upcoming Algebra test. In the days leading up to the test, you begin to badger your child about table manners, the cleanliness of their room, and not taking out the dog (i.e., the most important things to becoming a functional adult ☺), but in this moment they are distractions from the task at hand.

Rule #2 mentally cues the scene of Rebecca running down the tunnel after Coach Lasso screaming, "Beat them, Ted!" piling on more stress to his plate when he was already experiencing panic attacks.

---

[5] This term is derived from the behavior of seagulls, which are known for their abrupt and often aggressive interactions.

Where's Coach Beard when you need him? "Focus, baby!"

RULE #3
GET NAKED

Rule #3 is all about *Getting Naked* (the book by Patrick Lencioni, 100%). We think the writers of *Ted Lasso* could have had a lot of fun if they had chosen to give Lencioni's book to one of their players. (And Keeley would have been surprised when she walked into the locker room.) The title really means being vulnerable, which is a theme prevalent throughout the series.

We found that transparency in all of our business dealings was very effective in removing barriers and making for open and honest communication. "Getting Naked" became a theme for more than one webinar and presentation. (It was also a good way to drive attendance. ☺)

Jokes aside, there was one example where Ted wasn't transparent. He told his team he was dealing with stomach issues, instead of panic attacks. The team ultimately found out, which led to a brief trust issue – one that Ted handled (in a distinctly Ted-like way) with acknowledgment and discussion about trust. In the end, transparency and vulnerability are what solidify trust, which is a critical element of leadership.

Lasso clearly demonstrated vulnerability in later discussions about those panic attacks, his divorce, and not knowing a thing about what off-sides looked like. It allowed viewers and even reluctant Trent Crimm (James Lance) to root for him.

RULE #4
"ONWARD. FORWARD."

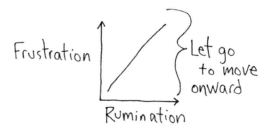

We are thankful to Ted for giving us the words for Rule #4 because Marnie likes to say, "Stop perseverating," which is just not as easy to understand (or say).

Ted eloquently points out that it is sometimes best to leave a mess in the rearview. Or if you have to relive it – like the coaches did in Season 2, Episode 9 (after losing badly to Manchester City in an important FA Cup match) – just watch the replay at 10x speed with the Benny Hill theme playing in the background.

Mistakes will happen. You must learn from them and move on. (Or ahem... "Be a goldfish." As Ted informed Sam, goldfish are the happiest animals on the planet because they have a 10-second memory.)

RULE #5
LEADERSHIP IS EARNED, NOT GIVEN

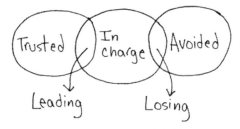

"Leadership is not about being in charge.
It is about taking care of those in your charge." —Simon Sinek

This quote by Simon Sinek emphasizes that effective leadership goes beyond holding a position of authority; it involves caring for and earning the trust and respect of those you lead. It suggests that true leaders don't rely solely on their title or position but instead lead by example and by building a genuine connection with their team or followers.

Early in his career, Nick really wished he had internalized Rule #5. He was promoted into a leadership position in a service delivery organization. His role changed from leading hands-on projects with small teams to leading an entire organization. Like many new leaders, he defaulted to "being in charge," but did not do enough to support his team members. He was too focused on his own insecurities, trying to prove he deserved the position. (Impostor Syndrome[6] for the win! Not!) Since then, Nick has held other leadership positions from VP of Engineering to VP of Customer Support... all the way to COO and Managing Partner. It would be nice if The Rules had an auto-correct feature, but alas, they do not. It took Nick some time to level up.

Not unlike the arc followed by characters in *Ted Lasso*, Nick's journey was an evolution. The result is that Rule #5 has become a core tenant of his personal operating system – *Take care of those in your charge!*

---

[6] Impostor Syndrome is a condition that causes one to feel like a fraud or a phony, despite tangible evidence to the contrary. It is characterized by self-doubt in one's intellect, skills, or accomplishments.

RULE #6
DEFEAT THE BLANK PAGE

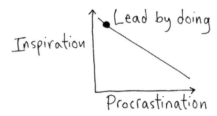

This has been a Rule that we reference monthly (at least!). It struck home early when shaping our business at Lifecycle Insights. We found our partners, prospects, and community members asked us the same questions around strategies for customer success. We decided to write a book on it. Writing any book (this one included) can be a daunting task. Even though you may have lots of ideas in your head, there's still a blank page in front of you.

We have found that the best way to get started is to just get started. That might sound cheeky, but it is a principle we live (and write books) by. Our first book started from a 30-minute freewriting experience, just brainstorming ideas onto a sheet of paper.

An interesting thing happens when you free-write. Your brain starts looking at those ideas and critiquing them and making them better. If you are beginning a project (and hoping to make it the best version it can be), you need to defeat that blank page!

Whether you are writing a blog post, reaching out to a new influencer, building a new module in a product, or even deciding what to make for dinner, getting something out on the table is critical for moving forward.

Rule #6A: Speed as a Habit

Once you start defeating the blank page easily, you will learn to iterate quickly. In the world of business, this helps you adapt to market changes. Personally, iterative approaches help you level up. When you aim to make yourself and your organization the best, leveling up is critical.

RULE #7
KILL 'EM WITH KINDNESS

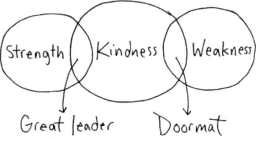

From the moment Ted stepped off the plane in London and insisted to Ollie (because of course Ted found out the name of his chauffeur) that he and Beard would carry their own luggage, Ted was nothing but nice. Heck, Rebecca even complained about how nice Ted was to AFC Richmond's Football Director, Higgins (played by Jeremy Swift).

The phrase "Don't take my kindness for weakness" serves as a vital companion to Ted Lasso's philosophy of leading with kindness. While Ted consistently demonstrates warmth and empathy, he also understands the importance of setting boundaries and maintaining assertiveness. It's a reminder that his compassionate leadership style is not a sign of naivety, but rather a conscious choice rooted in a deep understanding of human behavior.

Having run more than one support organization for companies, Nick could write an entire book on this Rule alone. When customers call with a complaint, issue, or concern, you can bet they always come in hot... but getting agitated, arguing back, or assigning blame is no way to address a situation. Nick learned early on that listening, validating their concern, apologizing (yes, try it, because it really works!), and helping others understand that you are there to help solve the problem is the best way to earn a great reputation as a company who cares about customer success. His support teams have awards to prove it (because nice guys and gals do not finish last ☺).

RULE #8
DON'T LET PERFECT BE THE ENEMY OF GOOD

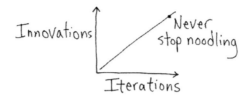

If you have any interest in starting a company, learn Rule #8. Otherwise, you could very well find yourself spinning your wheels. It's a cousin to Rule #6: Defeat the blank page. Many folks understand the struggle with getting something started, but another blocker is that once a project gets going, fear of failure can turn into a failure to launch. Too many people never let themselves take the risk.

While everyone would like to be perfect all of the time, the reality is that none of us are. The broader question is how to respond when you realize you aren't perfect.

When we first started our software company, we knew that we needed to test our product in the market before investing too much time and money. One of the processes we implemented to gather feedback was to host a weekly call. We invited all of our partners to this call and demonstrated new product features, then they gave us feedback. They were so excited to be involved in the process and be heard that they voluntarily tested our product and became constant sources of new feature requests.

We know that our customers helped our product become a better version because we did not attempt to wait to release a perfect product. Instead, we said, "This is good, so let's see how others can help make it better."

There is a fine line between sweating the small stuff (water pressure in showers, for example!) and trying to boil the ocean (something to be avoided at all costs).

What project do you have started that is stalled? Yeah... that one. What can you do to give it a little momentum and get it out the door?

RULE #9
CONQUER YOUR FEARS

(The Y-ps don't exist)

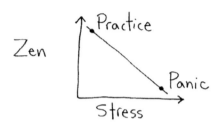

Let's look at how this Rule played a pivotal role in Dani Rojas's journey. After the devastating blow of a fatal penalty kick that killed Richmond's mascot, Earl the greyhound, Dani (played by Cristo Fernández) got "the Y-ps."[7] He could have easily succumbed to self-doubt. However, with the support of Ted Lasso, his fellow players, and team psychologist Dr. Sharon Fieldstone (Sarah Niles), Dani embraced Rule #9.

Dr. Sharon told Ted, "The yips are not a superstition; they are a mental condition. One that can be fixed with discipline... not denial." Dani took immediate action to rebuild his confidence and rediscovered his prowess on the pitch.

---

[7] (Are we even allowed to type it?) The "yips" is a term used in sports, particularly in golf, baseball, and sometimes in other activities like darts or cricket. It refers to a sudden and unexplained loss of fine motor skills and coordination, often resulting in a significant decline in performance. Athletes experiencing the yips might find it extremely difficult or even impossible to perform routine or previously automatic movements, such as making a putt in golf or throwing a ball accurately in baseball. This phenomenon is believed to have both physical and psychological components, and can be a highly frustrating and challenging experience for athletes who encounter it.

This transformation isn't just about skill; it's a testament to the power of taking action and maintaining a swift, adaptive approach. Dani's revival exemplifies how embracing the unwritten rules can lead to incredible growth and success, both in leadership and in life. (Really hoping it will help on the golf course!)

RULE #10
MANIFEST IT

(The Field of Dreams rule)

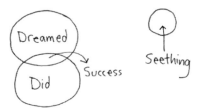

Build it and they will come. When Ted and his son Henry (Gus Turner) were playing Legos to create a double-decker bus, Ted's wife Michelle (Andrea Anders) came into the room and asked if they would rather go ride a real one. Henry answered that they needed to finish the Lego model first. Ted's response was, "Yeah, I get it. One of those 'build it before you ride it' scenarios."

We believe this rule holds true for culture, vision, and success. Manifesting what you want in this world isn't magic. It is about investing time and intention (and focus, baby!) to make it happen.

Influencers on every social media platform have quoted: "It took ten years to become an overnight success." Whether it's building a skill, developing a network, or creating a personal operating system that allows you to lead your life authentically, the manifestation of your dreams comes from putting in the work.

RULE #11
MAKE BUSINESS FUN

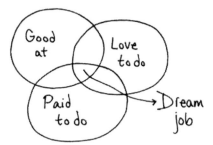

Ted made things fun; and the team bought in. Whether it was spelling "Hi, Boss" with human-formed letters or defeating the "Richmond Curse" via some silly ritual... the notion of fun acted as a pillar to the success of the team.

This book is a clear indicator of how we think business can be fun! When Marnie was assistant principal of a high school, she always coached students to find something they loved to do, and then do it well enough that someone would pay them to do it. We leveled up our own careers and built businesses where we could love what we do every day.

WRITING THE RULES

Along with the laughs (and tears) we got from *Ted Lasso*, we really walked away with a better understanding of how our Rules drive us as leaders for ourselves, our team, and our lives. We saw our own paths to leadership and how they paralleled many of the storylines in *Ted Lasso*.

Even when these rules were unwritten, we realized they impacted the way we ran our business. We also realized that because they had been unwritten, we missed the mark in communicating these rules.

When we hired our first employee (working remotely in the midst of the COVID-19 pandemic), we tried to communicate "the Lifecycle Insights way." We listed our core values on our website and had daily virtual conversations around business. Along with the primary core value of "developing raving fans" were "be transparent" and "get sh*t done." Our new hire had Dani's enthusiasm but not his determination – missed deadlines and miscommunications kept happening. Six months later when we had to let that person go, we reflected a lot on what we could have done better. We realized it came down to expectations. We had them, but our unwritten rules had remained undocumented, and it was hard to hold someone else accountable for expectations they didn't know we had.

So as hiring manager, Marnie created her Personal Operating System.[8] This included some helpful hints for communicating with Marnie and detailed her expectations.

Ted might appreciate this section from her document:

> *I aim to be positive and enthusiastic, bringing energy and passion to the space. I am one of those irritatingly chipper early risers who checks email at 5:15 AM. I cherish my morning hours of peace before the day begins so I can do thinking work and enjoy breakfast and tea with my husband before he goes to work. I will not bother you before 8 AM.*

Check out the full document at: **LeadItLikeLasso.com**

We took a stab at writing Ted's Personal Operating System. We suspect he would deliver this to new team members (along with a fresh box of biscuits).

---

[8] This idea originated when we found an article about Claire Hughes Johnson, leader at Stripe, who developed the idea of a "Working with me" document to share with her employees. We have since created our own framework, shared in Part Four, The Game, to help you build yours.

TED LASSO

- Gen X
- Football coach
- "The harder you work, the luckier you get"

PHILOSOPHY

If you're like me, you love a good locker room. It smells like potential. and I think we all have a lot of potential here. We are all about helping everyone become the best version of themselves. I've been called relentless and irritatingly nice. As your gaffer I believe it's my job to sweat the small stuff so you can focus on the big stuff like becoming the best player you can be.

MOTIVATION

I believe in believe. And if you believe in something, I want to hear it. You should know "I have a hard time hearing someone who doesn't believe in themselves" but as a player and leader on this team, we want to hear what you have to say.

DE-MOTIVATION

Pessimism, tea, bullies

LEADERSHIP POSITIONS

- Coach
- Father
- Dart club president

PERSONALITY

Patience

Analytical

Problem Solving

Handles Pressure

RICHMOND WAY

★★★★★ Belief

★★★☆☆ Conditioning

★★★★☆ Versatility

★★★★★ Awareness

FAVORITES/ CORE

LIBRARY

Wrinkle in Time, Coach Wooden's Pyramid of Success

Can you imagine Coach Beard's operating system? Or Roy's? We drafted some ideas and would love to have you add yours! Check them out at **LeadItLikeLasso.com.**

THINKING THROUGH THE RULES

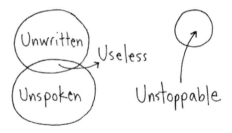

One of our team-building activities was to put new team members in the "hot seat" for a minute. We would fire off a range of questions from mild, medium, or hot... "Favorite concert?" "Favorite saying?"

Some hot seats were silly. Some were serious. All of them helped us better understand our new teammate. It was also a way to help our new teammate feel that we were inviting the whole human to our team, not just the part that would do the job. We believe this helps to create a safe space and build trust. It allows for connection, vulnerability, and communication to grow. Equally important, it gave us some conversation starters that helped us find similarities and differences. Just like the best soups, stews, and sauces... barbecue and otherwise... the best teams come as a result of having a variety of ingredients and spices. We were always looking for just the right blends.

PRO TIP: Liven things up at the dinner table tonight with this kind of hot seat activity (instead of the lecture-type).

We learned lots about our team during these activities. For example, we now know we all have strong opinions on whether or not a hotdog is a sandwich. But in our learning about company culture and through our experiences, what we have learned is that our personal rules – whether written or unwritten – impact our ability to work within an organization, be it a job or otherwise.

Companies have realized that while their culture is critical, how their culture aligns with their employees is just as crucial. When we get to Part Three's Training section, we are going to start with this idea because we find it extremely powerful. Every person needs to have a better understanding of their own rules in order to align themselves with jobs, activities, friends, and colleagues that, in fact, help them on their own path to becoming the best version of themselves.

Seriously...
is a hot dog
a sandwich?

But before that, since each *Ted Lasso* character enhanced the flavor of AFC Richmond (and helped us reflect on some of our own rules and values), we want to share how those personalities and personal operating systems can help you gain better insight into your own strengths and weaknesses. In Part Two, you get to take a good hard look at five of our favorite characters and see what lessons you can learn from them. Join us!

PART TWO

THE PLAYERS

2 THE PLAYERS

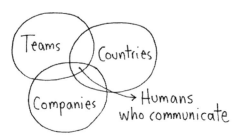

In the land of coaching, Ted Lasso never relied on one-size-fits-all strategies. He understood that to lead, you must know your team and yourself (thanks, Dr. Sharon Fieldstone) like you know the back of your hand – every quirk, every strength, and even the odd superstitions involving ghosts in the training room.

Much like Ted, we're about to learn a whole lot more about AFC Richmond (and life). As we do so, we'll dive into the heart of leadership, exploring how to identify and embrace the unique strengths within you and your team.

Think back to when Ted first met Sam Obisanya (played by Toheeb Jimoh). He didn't just see a talented athlete; he saw a young man with a profound connection to his homeland and a powerful drive to make a difference. So Ted nurtured that spark, helping Sam to flourish into a leader of his own accord.

Ted had to take several passes at figuring out Jamie Tartt's operating system – that is, before Keeley gave him that assist and suggested positive reinforcement.

Similarly, we're going to uncover those same hidden gems within you. Through this character leadership assessment, inspired by

Ted's keen insights, you'll discover which of the illustrious characters from the *Ted Lasso* universe resonates most with your own innate leadership style. Are you the resilient Roy Kent, the empathetic Sam Obisanya, the supportive Keeley Jones, the visionary Rebecca Welton, or perhaps even the indomitable Ted Lasso himself?

So, dear reader, grab your kit! The pitch is set. It's time to discover which character's leadership style aligns with your own.

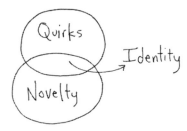

LEADERSHIP ASSESSMENT
DISCOVER YOUR INNER TED LASSO CHARACTER

Welcome to the Leadership Assessment that will help you uncover your leadership style and see how you can Lead It Like Lasso.

For each section, select two choices that resonate most for you.

Section 1: Core Values & Culture

A. My core values align with my team/family/company.

B. I consistently contribute to a culture of accountability.

C. I promote inclusivity and respect to nurture a positive environment.

D. I communicate the core values that are essential for the success of my organization.

E. I demonstrate adaptability to drive positive change in my organization.

*My choices:*_____ and _____

Section 2: Vision & Purpose

A. When faced with challenges, I focus on finding solutions and staying positive.

B. My leadership style involves tough love and pushing others to perform their best.

C. I believe in building strong relationships and fostering teamwork.

D. I'm driven by a clear vision and goals, and I'm not afraid of change.

E. My approach to leadership revolves around empathy and bringing out the best in people.

*My choices:*_____ and _____

Section 3: Communication & Influence

A. I communicate my ideas and vision clearly and with enthusiasm.

B. I'm direct and honest in communication, sometimes to the point of being blunt.

C. I prioritize active listening and building connections with my team.

D. I'm skilled at conveying a strategic plan and inspiring others to follow it.

E. I use positive reinforcement and encouragement to motivate my team.

*My choices:*_____ and _____

Section 4: Adaptability & Resilience

A. I handle crisis with optimism and a calm demeanor.

B. I approach challenges head-on and don't shy away from confrontations.

C. I adapt my leadership style to fit the needs of my team and the situation.

D. I'm open to change and see it as an opportunity for growth.

E. I maintain a resilient attitude and bounce back quickly from setbacks.

*My choices:*_____ and _____

Section 5: Collaboration & Team Building

A. I prioritize the success and well-being of my team over individual achievements.

B. I build strong connections with my team members and motivate them through tough times.

C. I foster an inclusive environment where everyone's ideas are valued.

D. I inspire my team by setting a strong example and sharing a compelling vision.

E. I connect with team members on a personal level and encourage their growth.

*My choices:*_____ and _____

Section 6: Leadership & Growth

A. I see leadership as serving others and putting their needs first.

B. I believe a tough-love approach is necessary to drive growth and success.

C. I empower my team members by providing guidance and opportunities for development.

D. I aim to transform my team and organization through strategic decisions.

E. I lead with optimism and inspire others to reach their potential.

*My choices:*_____ and _____

SCORING

Now tally how many times you selected each answer option:

A	B	C	D	E

Identify your 2 selections with the most tally marks.

Those will determine your spirit character. See legend below:

A	=	**Ted**
B	=	**Roy**
C	=	**Keeley**
D	=	**Rebecca**
E	=	**Sam**

Your Results:

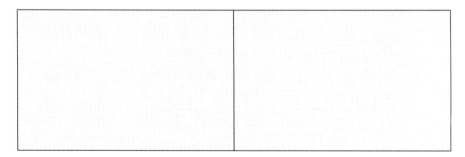

Now that you know which characters align with your personality traits, let's dive into the strengths and opportunities for growth in leadership styles for each character.

SAM OBISANYA
"THE OPTIMISTIC ACHIEVER"

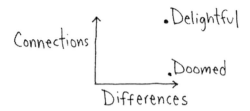

Ahh, sweet Sam Obisanya. Sam is the Nigerian superstar on the pitch who wears his heart on his sleeve... and his political views *not* on his jersey. Who doesn't love Sam? (Did you know Roy Kent actor Brett Goldstein uses a picture of Sam as the wallpaper on his cellphone?)

Sam embodies the role of the optimistic achiever with remarkable finesse and a sparkling smile. His leadership style is characterized by an unwavering positivity that radiates through every aspect of his interactions with teammates and coaches. Sam is a source of inspiration, always able to find the silver lining even in the most challenging situations. His enthusiasm and genuine belief in the team's potential serve as powerful motivators for those around him.

As an achiever, Sam sets high standards for himself and tirelessly works toward his goals. He demonstrates an exceptional work ethic both on and off the field, setting an example for his teammates to emulate. His determination and relentless pursuit of excellence, as well as his eagerness to learn, make him a natural leader. His actions speak volumes about his commitment to the team's success.

> *Sam's enthusiasm and belief are powerful motivators.*

One of Sam's key strengths lies in his ability to uplift others. He is all about the team. He was the one who finally broke the team-activity stalemate when they spent the night in Amsterdam... by suggesting a pillow fight.

37

He's quick to acknowledge the efforts of his teammates and offer encouragement when it's needed most. This fosters a sense of camaraderie and unity, creating a positive and supportive team environment that is conducive to growth and success.

Sam's leadership style is a testament to the transformative power of optimism and hard work. He exemplifies the belief that with the right attitude and a relentless pursuit of one's goals, even the loftiest aspirations can be achieved. His presence on the field and within the team dynamic is a driving force that propels everyone to greater heights of achievement. Sam's humility in the face of success demonstrates that remaining grounded and grateful is vital for continued growth.

If your personal assessment aligned with Sam, you might recognize some of these traits in your own abilities. And if you didn't score like Sam at all, then you might seek to develop some of these characteristics.

◊ **Embrace Positivity**: Sam learned to be a "goldfish." He shook off his mistakes and embraced a positive outlook.

◊ **Perseverance Pays Off**: Remember the time Sam overcame doubts to become a key player? His journey teaches us the value of consistency and hard work.

◊ **Embrace Learning Opportunities**: When Sam faced criticism, he turned it into motivation. Embrace feedback and use it to better yourself.

◊ **Be a Role Model**: Sam's ability to inspire his teammates shows that leading by example can create a positive and motivated environment.

◊ **Stay Humble**: Sam's humility in the face of success demonstrates that remaining grounded and grateful is vital for continued growth.

No one is perfect, however. Sam might need to work on his self-discipline and his ability to adapt to various leadership situations. He could benefit from honing his assertiveness to be able to express his opinions and ideas, ensuring his voice is heard in crucial team discussions.

Additionally, developing strategic thinking and long-term planning could enhance Sam's ability to anticipate challenges and steer the team toward sustained success.

Lastly, refining his conflict-resolution skills would empower Sam to navigate disagreements, fostering a more harmonious and productive working environment. If you are like Sam, remember Rule #7. You can kill them with kindness, but they should not mistake your kindness for weakness.

If you see some of yourself in Sam and want to work on those weaknesses, here are a few tactics to consider:

◊ Develop a daily routine that includes focused work periods to improve self-discipline.

◊ Seek mentorship from experienced leaders to understand how they adapt to different situations.

◊ Attend workshops or courses to enhance your strategic thinking and decision-making skills.

◊ Practice assertive communication to effectively express your ideas and opinions.

◊ Embrace failure as a learning opportunity, and apply lessons to future endeavors.

One of our favorite scenes in *Ted Lasso* was when Ted gifted each of the players a book. Those titles were hand-picked to help them become the best version of themselves. If Ted continued that tradition, here are a few he might recommend for Sam (or those who want to be more like Sam):

From Sam's Bookshelf

Quiet: The Power of Introverts in a World That Can't Stop Talking
Susan Cain

To reinforce Sam's leadership strengths and contributions as a more introverted team member, ultimately fostering a more inclusive and effective work environment.

The Measure of Our Success: A Letter to My Children and Yours
Marian Wright Edelman

To help Sam get insights into defining purpose and setting meaningful goals, aligning with his sense of vision and purpose.

Atomic Habits: An Easy & Proven Way to Build Good Habits & Break Bad Ones
James Clear

To help Sam reinforce strong habits that can be repeated for improving everyday life.

ROY KENT
"THE TOUGH-LOVE MENTOR"

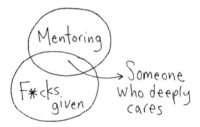

"He's here! He's there! He's every-f*cking-where, Roy Kent!" Three episodes in, Marnie walked into her house to see her 22-year-old daughter jumping around shouting this cheer like a lifelong AFC Richmond fan. Showing grit and vulnerability in an Oscar-the-Grouch-like demeanor, Roy gave fans a lot to cheer for.

Roy Kent embodies the role of the tough-love mentor in *Ted Lasso* with a no-nonsense approach that is both impactful and effective. His leadership style is characterized by a straightforwardness that leaves no room for ambiguity. Roy is unafraid to confront challenges head-on (literally... he might head butt you), offering candid feedback and constructive criticism when needed. This directness, although ~~occasionally~~ almost always gruff, stems from a commitment to the team's success and the belief that accountability is paramount.

> *Roy's tough love is rooted in a genuine desire to see his teammates reach their full potential.*

As a mentor, Roy's tough love is rooted in a genuine desire to see his teammates reach their full potential. He recognizes that, sometimes, pushing people out of their comfort zone is necessary for growth. His high expectations reflect his confidence in the abilities of those around him and his firm belief that they are capable of achieving greatness.

Roy's leadership style also emphasizes leading by example. His dedication to the sport and the team is evident in every aspect of his conduct, setting a standard for work ethic and commitment that his teammates admire and strive to emulate. His willingness to put in the hard work and make personal sacrifices for the betterment of the team reinforces the value of selflessness and dedication.

In essence, Roy Kent's tough-love mentorship style is a driving force behind the team's progression. While it may be demanding, it stems from a genuine desire to see his teammates succeed, pushing them to become the best versions of themselves both on and off the pitch. His approach, although stern, ultimately fosters a culture of accountability and growth within the team.

Do you see yourself in Roy? These might be some of your superpowers:

◊ **Own Your Strengths**: Roy's unapologetic nature shows us that recognizing and embracing our strengths is essential for effective leadership.

◊ **Authenticity Matters**: Roy's candidness teaches us that authenticity fosters genuine relationships and trust with team members.

◊ **Balance Intensity with Empathy**: Despite his tough exterior, Roy's compassion for Keeley and his niece, Phoebe, illustrates that leadership involves understanding emotions.

◊ **Provide Constructive Criticism**: Roy's ability to offer honest feedback, like he did with Jamie and Isaac, demonstrates the value of constructive criticism for growth.

◊ **Lead with Integrity**: Roy's decision to prioritize the team over his own ego exemplifies the importance of ethical leadership.

While Roy Kent's tough-love mentorship style is effective, there are areas where he could refine his leadership skills.

First, he might benefit from incorporating more empathy into his approach, allowing him to connect on a deeper level with his teammates and understand their individual motivations and struggles. Dialing up his emotional intelligence (known as Emotional Quotient, or EQ for short) would complement his impressive football IQ.

Second, developing more patience and tolerance for mistakes could help him navigate moments of adversity with greater composure and understanding.

Finally, honing his ability to delegate tasks and trust in the capabilities of his teammates could lead to a more efficient and harmonious team dynamic, allowing each member to contribute their strengths effectively.

Here are some tactics that might help a Roy Kent-like leader:

◊ Participate in team-building activities to build stronger relationships with colleagues. (But ahem, we do *not* recommend Roy's "string" bonding activity.)

◊ Dedicate time to personal development (maybe you also have never learned to ride a bike?) and explore ways to cultivate a more positive attitude.

◊ Attend workshops on effective communication to improve your feedback delivery.

◊ Set aside time for brainstorming sessions with your team to encourage creativity.

◊ Delegate tasks that play to your team members' strengths, demonstrating trust in their abilities.

From Roy's Bookshelf

Radical Candor: Be a Kick-Ass Boss Without Losing Your Humanity
Kim Scott

To help Roy balance his tough-love approach with empathy, fostering better communication and understanding.

Extreme Ownership: How U.S. Navy SEALs Lead and Win
Jocko Willink and Leif Babin

The mindset that allows Navy SEALs (and peak athletes) to succeed can also be applied to Roy's leadership... like "Cover and Move," "Decentralized Command," and "Leading Up the Chain."

Emotional Intelligence 2.0
Travis Bradberry and Jean Greaves

Knowing what EQ is and employing it are two entirely different beasts. Roy could learn how to use the skills of self-awareness, self-management, social awareness, and relationship management to achieve his fullest potential as a leader and a human.

KEELEY JONES
"THE SUPPORTIVE COLLABORATOR"

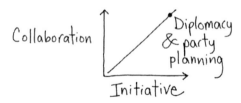

Yeah, Keeley Jones is cute as a button and can rhyme her bum off. These aren't the only things she has going for her. Anyone who can warm the cold, bitter heart of divorcée Rebecca Welton clearly has the EQ of a great leader.

Keeley Jones embodies the role of a supportive collaborator in *Ted Lasso*, demonstrating a leadership style characterized by her unwavering dedication to the team's success. Her approach is marked by a genuine warmth, honesty (less brutal than Roy's), and a deep sense of care for those in her network. Keeley goes out of her way to foster a positive and inclusive team environment, recognizing the value of unity and mutual respect. She excels at building strong relationships with each member, providing them with the support and encouragement they need to excel.

As a collaborator, Keeley actively seeks out opportunities for teamwork and collective problem-solving. She understands the power of leveraging diverse perspectives and skill sets, fostering an environment where every member feels heard and valued. Her ability to bring out the best in others is a testament to her belief in the collective strength of the team.

> *Keeley's positive reinforcement instills a sense of pride and camaraderie within the group.*

Keeley's leadership style also emphasizes the importance of celebrating wins and acknowledging the efforts of her teammates. This positive reinforcement serves as a powerful motivator, instilling a sense of pride and camaraderie within the group. Keeley's ability to lift spirits

45

and boost morale, even in challenging moments, contributes significantly to the team's overall cohesion and resilience.

In essence, Keeley Jones's supportive collaborator leadership style is a driving force behind the team's unity and success. Her genuine care for her teammates, coupled with an emphasis on teamwork and celebration, creates an environment where every member feels empowered to contribute their best. Keeley's approach fosters a culture of inclusivity and mutual support, laying the foundation for a thriving and high-performing team.

Are you a Keeley? Regardless of your rhyming skills, some of these might feel like you:

◊ **Build Strong Relationships**: Keeley's role as a glue that binds the team highlights the significance of building meaningful connections.

◊ **Foster a Positive Environment**: Keeley's influence on the team's camaraderie underlines that nurturing positivity can lead to a more productive workspace.

◊ **Encourage Each Other**: Keeley's support for all of AFC Richmond reminds us that leadership is about empowering others to achieve greatness.

◊ **Be a Team Player**: Keeley's willingness to collaborate with Coach Lasso shows that leaders should be team players who value collective effort.

◊ **Seek Opportunities for Growth**: Keeley's journey from influencer to PR consultant to startup entrepreneur illustrates that embracing new challenges can lead to personal and professional growth.

While Keeley Jones excels in her role as a supportive collaborator, there are areas in which she could further enhance her leadership skills.

First, she might benefit from developing a more assertive communication style, allowing her to express her ideas and concerns with greater confidence. This could empower her to take charge in crucial moments and ensure her voice is heard effectively.

Additionally, honing her decision-making abilities and taking initiative in challenging situations could further solidify her role as a trusted leader within the team.

Keeley excels at building relationships. (Although you shouldn't be so loyal to friends that they bring goats into the office to try to ruin you!) She might further enhance her leadership by targeting her strategic thinking to align her collaborative efforts with larger organizational goals.

Maybe some of these ideas have made it into Keeley's unicorn notebook:

◊ Develop a clear vision for your team and communicate it consistently.

◊ Attend courses on goal-setting and action planning to enhance your leadership skills.

◊ Set up regular one-on-one meetings with team members to discuss their aspirations and growth.

◊ Seek opportunities to take the lead on cross-functional projects to expand your influence.

◊ Practice presenting your ideas in a compelling and persuasive manner.

From Keeley's Bookshelf

Dare to Lead: Brave Work. Tough Conversations. Whole Hearts.
Brené Brown

To empower Keeley to lead with vulnerability and encourage a culture of openness within her collaborative approach.

The Art of Gathering: How We Meet and Why It Matters
Priya Parker

This book focuses on creating meaningful connections and fostering a sense of togetherness, mirroring Keeley's strength in building relationships and collaboration.

Buy Back Your Time
Dan Martell

This book focuses on strategies to "get unstuck, reclaim your freedom, and build your empire." This could save Keeley from the burnout she had as she started her marketing firm KJPR.

REBECCA WELTON
"THE VISIONARY TRANSFORMER"

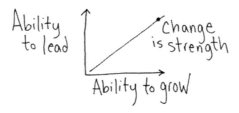

Team owner Rebecca Welton is a force to be reckoned with. Her personal growth across the three seasons of the series directly impacts her football club. We are curious how many people have now stood in front of a mirror and made themselves as big as possible to develop the confidence that Rebecca exudes.

Time out: Rebecca only started out as a bitter, spiteful human. Part of the magic of Ted Lasso's "biscuits with the boss" and Keeley's "girl talk" was how Rebecca really grew into the leader she always could be. So we ask that you remember the Season 3 version of Rebecca here: the Boss-ass Bitch (as Sassy's daughter likes to call her ☺!)

Rebecca embodies the role of a visionary transformer in the series, showcasing a leadership style driven by her clear vision and transformative approach. As the owner of AFC Richmond, she is unwavering in her commitment to redefine the team's trajectory. Rebecca's visionary mindset is evident in her ability to see beyond immediate challenges and envision a future of success for the club. She sets ambitious goals and tirelessly works toward them, inspiring those around her to share in her vision.

Rebecca's transformational leadership style is marked by a willingness to challenge the status quo. She's unafraid of change, recognizing it as a necessary step to growth and improvement. Her strategic decisions and bold initiatives aim to revolutionize the team's culture and performance. By instigating shifts in mindset and behavior, Rebecca fosters an environment of continuous improvement and adaptability.

Furthermore, Rebecca places immense value on cultivating a culture of accountability and excellence. She holds herself and her team to high standards, encouraging them to strive for nothing short of their best. Her unwavering belief in the potential of AFC Richmond serves as a driving force behind the team's journey toward greatness.

> *Rebecca's transformational leadership is marked by a willingness to challenge the status quo.*

In essence, Rebecca Welton's visionary transformer leadership style is instrumental in AFC Richmond's pursuit of success. Her ability to articulate a compelling vision, drive transformational change, and demand excellence from her team establishes her as a powerful and influential leader. Rebecca's leadership style leaves an indelible mark on the club, setting them on a path to a brighter and more prosperous future.

If Rebecca (after several episodes of biscuits with the boss and girl talk with Keeley) resonates for you, then here are some strengths that might align with your leadership style:

◊ **Communicate a Clear Vision**: Rebecca's efforts to redefine the club's image teaches us the importance of articulating a compelling vision.

◊ **Lead with Confidence**: Rebecca's leadership journey, even as she faced doubts, demonstrates that confidence is key to inspiring others.

◊ **Adaptability Matters**: Rebecca's ability to pivot and lead in various situations shows us that adaptability is crucial for successful leadership.

◊ **Value Collaboration**: Rebecca's partnership with Keeley and Ted showcases the power of collaborative leadership for achieving ambitious goals.

◊ **Embrace Change**: Rebecca's transformation from a controlling owner to a more open leader highlights the importance of embracing change for growth.

While Rebecca Welton is undoubtedly a visionary transformer, there are areas where she could further refine her leadership approach.

First, fostering a more collaborative and inclusive environment could amplify her team's collective efforts toward achieving the club's goals. Actively seeking input and valuing diverse perspectives can lead to more comprehensive decision-making.

Additionally, finding a balance between assertiveness and empathy in her leadership style would help build stronger relationships with team members, enhancing overall cohesion within AFC Richmond.

Here are some "training" activities Rebecca might want to consider:

◊ Invest time in fostering a positive and collaborative team culture through team-building activities.

◊ Attend leadership workshops to improve conflict resolution and mediation skills.

◊ Develop a mentorship program within the organization to facilitate employee growth.

◊ Engage in strategic planning sessions to align your vision with the long-term goals of the company. (Rebecca and Higgins could work on Keeley's new proposal.)

◊ Actively seek feedback from your team and peers to refine your leadership style.

From Rebecca's Bookshelf

Leading Change
John P. Kotter

To equip Rebecca with strategies for leading successful organizational transformations while maintaining focus on her vision.

Black Titan: A.G. Gaston and the Making of a Black American Millionaire
Carol Jenkins and Elizabeth Gardner Hines

This biography of A.G. Gaston highlights his vision and transformative impact, resonating with Rebecca's drive to reshape the team and her commitment to change.

Good to Great: Why Some Companies Make the Leap and Others Don't
Jim Collins

Rebecca's transformation from controlling owner to open leader could be enriched by incorporating humility, acknowledging her own limitations, and valuing the contributions of others.

TED LASSO
"THE POSITIVITY GURU"

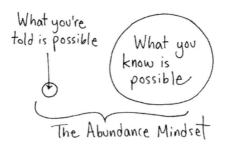

The world adored Ted Lasso... but what they really fell in love with was how Ted made them feel. There are podcasts, social media fan groups, blog posts, books, t-shirts, mugs... and even a Twitter account just for his mustache. Everyone wants to be Ted or work for Ted.

Ted Lasso's leadership style, often referred to as "the positivity guru," is characterized by an unwavering optimism, genuine care for his team, and an innate ability to inspire others. He approaches challenges with a can-do attitude, focusing on finding solutions rather than dwelling on problems. Ted believes in the power of positive thinking and its impact on team morale and performance. His infectious enthusiasm uplifts spirits, creating a motivating environment for everyone involved.

One of Ted's standout leadership traits is his exceptional ability to connect with individuals on a personal level. He loves meeting somebody's mom... "because it is like getting a glimpse into why they're crazy." He takes the time

> *Ted takes the time to understand everyone's unique strengths, struggles, and aspirations.*

to understand their unique strengths, struggles, and aspirations, tailoring his guidance accordingly. This fosters a deep sense of trust and respect between Ted and his team members. Ted's emphasis on building strong relationships creates a supportive foundation for collaboration and teamwork.

Furthermore, Ted places a strong emphasis on continuous growth and development, not only for himself but for his entire team. He encourages a growth mindset, celebrating both individual and collective achievements. Ted's leadership style extends beyond the soccer field, emphasizing the importance of personal growth and wellbeing. His focus on "helping these gentlemen become the best versions of themselves" ultimately contributes to the team's success.

In essence, Ted Lasso's leadership style revolves around creating an environment where positivity, connection, and growth flourish. His ability to inspire and uplift those around him is a driving force behind AFC Richmond's journey toward greatness. Ted's leadership approach demonstrates that a positive outlook and genuine care can lead to exceptional teamwork, performance, and overall success.

Where do you see yourself in Ted's style? Do you do any of the following:

◊ **Cultivate Positivity**: Ted's endless optimism demonstrates the impact of maintaining a positive outlook even in challenging circumstances.

◊ **Show Empathy**: Ted's empathy toward Jamie Tartt's struggles teaches us the importance of understanding and supporting team members.

◊ **Believe in People**: Ted's belief in the potential of each individual, like Nate the Great, shows us the power of unlocking hidden talents.

◊ **Adapt and Inspire**: Ted's willingness to adapt to a new sport and inspire a soccer team transcends his comfort zone, illustrating the value of flexibility.

◊ **Lead with Kindness**: Ted's kindness to everyone, including nay-sayers, reminds us that kindness can create a positive, collaborative, and successful environment.

While Ted Lasso excels in many aspects of leadership, there are areas where he could further enhance his effectiveness.

First, focusing his strategic thinking and long-term planning would provide a more structured direction for AFC Richmond. This could involve developing a clear roadmap and setting specific, measurable goals to guide the team's progress.

Additionally, refining conflict resolution skills could help Ted navigate challenging situations with even greater finesse, ensuring that any conflicts are addressed constructively and in a way that promotes team unity.

Ted also needs to work on self-care. He was so intent on helping everyone else that he didn't work on himself until stricken by panic attacks.

Maybe while Ted is back in the States, he can take a look at some of these strategies to work on his skills (and you can join along!):

◊ Enroll in decision-making workshops to enhance strategic approach.

◊ Attend courses on setting measurable goals that align with an optimistic outlook.

◊ Develop a plan for handling tough conversations with empathy and understanding.

◊ Practice presenting a positive vision to different stakeholders to rally support.

◊ Collaborate with peers to enhance your adaptability and flexibility in leadership.

From Ted's Bookshelf

Leaders Eat Last: Why Some Teams Pull Together and Others Don't
Simon Sinek

To further reinforce Ted's emphasis on teamwork, trust, and leading with a servant's heart.

The Power of Positive Thinking
Norman Vincent Peale

This classic work on positivity and optimism aligns with Ted's philosophy of turning challenges into opportunities and leading with a positive mindset.

The Mountain Is You: Transforming Self-Sabotage into Self-Mastery
Brianna Wiest

This work would help Ted to do the self-care and internal work needed to build resilience.

As we considered each of the characters, we could see traits from several that had us reflecting on our own strengths and weaknesses. We would love to hear from all the front-stage Teds and Rebeccas out there, and the hardcore Roys and kind-hearted Sams and Keeleys.

If you want to explore more about your leadership style or share other ideas (maybe you are a Higgins or a Trent Crimm!), head over to **LeadItLikeLasso.com** to continue the conversation.

LEADERS LIKE LASSO, IRL[9]

If the internet is any indication, then it is a popular view that we could use more people like Ted Lasso in our lives. That realization inspired us to look around and consider some modern-day leaders who align with this leadership assessment.

We took the liberty of characterizing a few. (We can't wait to hear your suggestions! And if any of these leaders are reading this book, let us know how we did!)

Ted Lasso: Positive and Encouraging Leader

IRL: **Oprah Winfrey**, Media Mogul, Philanthropist, and TV Personality

Oprah Winfrey is known for her positive and uplifting approach to leadership. She emphasizes empowerment, encouragement, and personal growth, much like Coach Lasso does on the pitch and in the locker room.

Ted Lasso and Oprah Winfrey both embody the essence of positive and encouraging leadership, albeit in different contexts and industries.

Known for his affable and optimistic demeanor, Ted brings a unique approach to coaching in the world of professional soccer. He exudes positivity, always seeking to uplift and motivate his team, even in the face of challenges. Ted's infectious enthusiasm and unwavering belief in his players' potential create a supportive environment that

---

[9] IRL = In real life.

fosters growth and camaraderie. His leadership style demonstrates the power of positivity in driving individuals to level up.

Oprah Winfrey, a media mogul and philanthropist, is renowned for her ability to inspire and uplift millions. Her leadership is characterized by empathy, authenticity, and a genuine desire to help others discover their own potential. Oprah's talk show, in particular, became a platform for sharing stories of triumph over adversity and offering a message of hope. Through her own journey and the stories she brings to light, Oprah embodies the idea that positivity and encouragement can be transformative forces.

While Ted Lasso's leadership plays out on the soccer field and in the locker room, and Oprah's influence extends across media and philanthropy, both share a common commitment to positive and uplifting leadership. They remind us of the profound impact that encouragement and positivity can have in empowering individuals to reach their highest potential.

Rebecca Welton: Resilient and Determined Leader

IRL: **Walt Disney**, Creator of Disney World

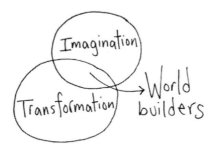

Walt Disney and Rebecca Welton, though from vastly different backgrounds and industries, share a common bond. Both exemplify the visionary transformer archetype.

Rebecca Welton hails from the world of professional sports, where her role as AFC Richmond's owner demands strategic thinking and a transformative mindset. Rebecca's original decision to hire Ted clearly had ulterior motives. However, her decision to keep him, an unconventional choice by any standard, demonstrates a willingness to challenge the status quo. Rebecca's vision for the team goes beyond mere wins and losses; she aspires to create a culture of growth and camaraderie, transcending boundaries of traditional sports management. In this regard, she mirrors Disney's audacity to rewrite the rules and craft a legacy that extends far beyond the field.

Walt Disney was a pioneer in the entertainment industry, renowned for his creative genius and ability to envision new worlds. He dared to challenge the norms of animation, introducing innovations like synchronized sound and color, which revolutionized the film industry. His unwavering belief in the power of imagination led to the creation of Disneyland, a theme park that redefined the concept of immersive storytelling. Like Rebecca, Disney's visionary approach sought to transform his industry and bring joy to millions through imaginative experiences.

While their arenas of influence differ, both Walt Disney and Rebecca embody the spirit of visionary transformation. They remind us that leadership transcends industries, and at its core, it's about having the courage to envision a future that defies conventional wisdom.

Keeley Jones: Relationship-Oriented Leader

IRL: **Richard Branson**, Founder of Virgin Group

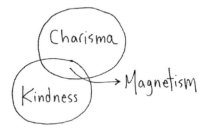

Richard Branson is known for his personable and relationship-driven leadership style. He prioritizes building strong connections with employees, customers, and partners, much like Keeley's emphasis on relationships.

Keeley Jones, a media influencer, and Richard Branson, the renowned entrepreneur and founder of Virgin Group, both exhibit relationship-oriented leadership styles in their respective domains.

Keeley Jones is portrayed as a supportive collaborator who places emphasis on building and nurturing relationships with those around her. Whether it's her friendships with fellow characters or her role as a supportive partner to Roy Kent, Keeley exemplifies the importance of human connection and mutual support in achieving common goals. Her ability to foster teamwork and camaraderie reflects her relationship-oriented approach to leadership.

Richard Branson, known for his charismatic and people-centric leadership style, places a premium on building meaningful relationships with employees, customers, and partners. His emphasis on creating a positive work environment and treating employees with respect has contributed to the success of Virgin Group. Branson's approach to leadership is characterized by his genuine interest in people and his belief in the power of strong relationships to drive organizational success.

Both Keeley Jones and Richard Branson exemplify relationship-oriented leadership. They recognize the significance of building trust, fostering collaboration, and valuing the contributions of those with whom they work. Their examples highlight the impact of strong interpersonal connections in achieving shared objectives and creating a positive organizational culture.

Sam Obisanya: Growth-Minded Leader

IRL: **Satya Nadella**, CEO of Microsoft

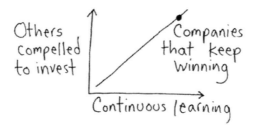

Satya Nadella is recognized for his growth-minded and innovative approach to leadership. He has transformed Microsoft's culture by emphasizing a growth mindset, empathy, and inclusivity.

Sam Obisanya and Satya Nadella both embody growth-minded leadership, albeit in different contexts and industries.

Sam is portrayed as an optimistic achiever who believes in continuous self-improvement. He approaches challenges with a positive mindset, seeking solutions and focusing on personal growth. His willingness to learn from setbacks and his dedication to becoming the best version of himself align with the principles of growth-minded leadership.

Like Sam, Satya Nadella is an optimistic leader who sets high standards. He believes in the potential for positive change and improvement, even in challenging situations. As the CEO of Microsoft, Nadella is a strategic thinker who focuses on the long-term vision and goals of the company. He has led them through significant transformations and strategic shifts.

Both Sam Obisanya and Satya Nadella demonstrate a growth-oriented approach to leadership. They believe in the power of continuous learning, development, and adaptability as essential elements for personal and professional growth. Their examples serve as inspiration for aspiring leaders looking to cultivate a growth mindset in their own journeys.

Roy Kent: Direct and Assertive Leader

IRL: **Nick Saban**, Head Coach, University of Alabama football

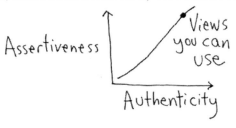

Nick Saban, much like Roy Kent, is known for his direct and assertive leadership style. He's unafraid to make bold decisions and set clear expectations, reflecting Roy's straightforward approach both on and off the field. Despite working in different sports, both Saban and Kent share a common thread of directness and assertiveness in their leadership styles.

Roy Kent, a seasoned professional athlete turned coach, is known for his no-nonsense approach. He doesn't mince words and is unapologetically straightforward in his communication. His assertiveness stems from a deep-seated passion for the game and a desire to see his team succeed. Roy's leadership style is grounded in a firm belief in accountability and pushing individuals to perform at their best. His directness is a reflection of his commitment to achieving results.

Nick Saban, a highly successful and respected U.S. football coach, is renowned for his no-nonsense approach to coaching. He sets high standards for his players and expects nothing less than their absolute best. Saban's assertiveness comes from a deep understanding of the game and a relentless pursuit of excellence. His direct communication style is rooted in an unwavering commitment to achieving success.

While Roy Kent and Nick Saban operate in vastly different domains (European football versus American football ☺), they both exemplify direct and assertive leadership. Their styles may manifest in different ways, but the underlying principle remains the same –

a resolute commitment to their vision and a willingness to lead with unwavering conviction.

Each of these real-life leaders shares key traits with the *Ted Lasso* characters, demonstrating their respective leadership profiles in their own domains. They didn't just get to where they are overnight. It took a bit of practice. Now let's dive into The Training!

PART THREE

THE
TRAINING

3 THE TRAINING

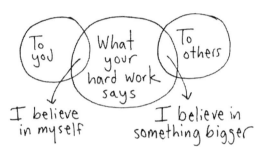

Previously on Ted Lasso...

Ted chews out Jamie Tartt in the locker room because Jamie said he couldn't practice. Ted is addressing Jamie's lack of commitment to the team and his unwillingness to fully engage in training. Ted emphasizes the importance of putting in the effort and working together as a team for the greater good. He holds Jamie accountable for his actions and challenges him to consider the impact of his behavior on the entire team.

This scene references the real-world rant of the all-star basketball player Allen Iverson. He famously made a statement at a press conference downplaying the significance of practice, which led to criticism and controversy. Both situations highlight the tension between individual talent and teamwork. They underscore the importance of recognizing that even the most talented individuals need to be committed to practicing and working together with their teammates to achieve success.

How does that relate to "practice" and "leadership"? The good news, as reported by the renowned business consulting group McKinsey, is that leadership is not an ability you are born with. This means it is a skill that can be taught. The (potentially) bad news is that leadership requires you to put in the work (i.e., practice).

More good news! Roy Kent isn't going to show up at your door at 4:00 AM, yelling at you to start your training, but it is still going to take some effort. As they say: "Hard work beats talent, if talent doesn't work hard."

So what is it that you need to practice? Well, as was very clear on *Ted Lasso*, it depends on where you are now, and where you want to be.

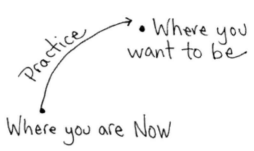

If you follow any of the commentary on social media from the creators of *Ted Lasso*, you will hear talk of their characters and story "arc."

Here's AFC Richmond's "arc" from Season 1 to Season 3:

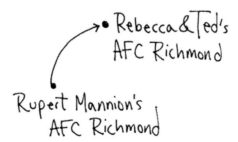

That simple graphic makes it look easy, doesn't it?

The reality looked more like this:

It's pretty clear that reality can be messy, but we suspect you already knew that. Yet it doesn't change the fact that if you have a vision for where you want to go, and a plan for how to get there, with the skill, the will, and the team, you can absolutely make it happen.

What is it that *you* are making happen? Well, that very much depends on you. Where is it that you want to level up in how you lead in your life?

◊   Are you running a company?

◊   Are you leading a team?

◊   Are you trying to find a job you would love?

◊   Are you helping your kids become the best versions of themselves?

Maybe you can answer yes to all of the above. Regardless of whether you are reading this for business or personal reasons, we are going to outline the components of leadership that will get you where you want to go.

We have read a lot of leadership advice; we've reviewed leadership course syllabi; we've devoured countless books devoted to the topic; we've even read college-level leadership textbooks. Though organized a bit differently, they all contain similar elements. One thing that sticks out is that many of them start with an overview of *leadership*, and then dive into *vision* and *purpose*. Somewhere along the way there might be a section, or for the more modern books, maybe even an entire chapter about *culture* and *core values.*

When we stopped to think about what elements we wanted to include in *Lead It Like Lasso*, we took a good hard look at how we ourselves started our company. What we learned is that we focused on our core values first. We'll dive into that a lot more in the next chapter, but Core Values & Culture is our first essential element to leadership.

As we've said many times, if you are building a business or trying to lose weight or aiming to find the job of your dreams, that is all based on Vision & Purpose, which follows closely behind Core Values & Culture. In order to get there, there are three other essential elements to make the magic happen. Success also depends on Communication & Influence, Network & Community, and finally having an eye toward Legacy and Growth.

So let's get to it!

We will look at examples from *Ted Lasso,* of course, but also from real-life modern leaders in business today. (You might try to stop Marnie from throwing in a story or two, but Nick couldn't, so you will find some of our stories too!) Most importantly, however, is for you to think through the elements and the stories presented here, then take a look at how these elements play a role in you leading your own life... so you can practice!

4 CORE VALUES & CULTURE

Okay, we have waited on this pun long enough...

We *mustache* you a question:

> If Trent Crimm spent two years embedded in your organization
> (or family), documenting everything, what would be the title of
> the book he writes about it?

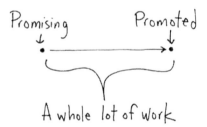

Flashback to the Season 3 finale when Trent Crimm shares his
manuscript for *The Lasso Way*. Not so surprising, Ted's only
feedback was that the book should be renamed *The Richmond
Way*... "because it never was about me anyway." There isn't a fan
who watched that episode who wouldn't want to read such a book.

This feedback alone was indicative of the humility with which Ted
led his life and his club. But before we dig further into some of Ted's
other traits and core values, let's talk about what that book title
could have meant to Trent Crimm.

Ted took a team from relegation to a final match for the championship. Yet Trent didn't opt to write any of these books:

◊ *Strategies and Tactics of Winning Football*

◊ *The Lasso Special: 10 Trick Plays for the Win*

◊ *Best Skills and Drills for a Championship Football Team*

We believe Trent saw what Ted was trying to tell him from the very beginning. It wasn't strategies and tactics that were going to help AFC Richmond succeed. It was building up every individual and the culture of the entire club to work as a team. That is really what Ted was getting at when he surprised Trent with this nugget:

> *"It isn't about the wins and losses.*
> *It is about helping these young men*
> *become the best versions of themselves."*

Ted believed, and we agree, that no amount of training, drills, wind sprints, or penalty kick practice would have allowed AFC Richmond to be successful if they didn't also build the proper culture of teamwork and support.

As we reflected on this idea and on how we started our company, we realized that for us too, the core values came first – even before the vision and mission of the company. So let's start there!

OUR CORE VALUES

Thanks to the magic of social media, we recently watched a 2023 graduation speech from North Carolina State given by a young lady named Kelsey O'Connor. She had been a scholarship softball player with a career-ending head injury. She then struggled to find her identity. She always thought of herself as a "softball player." She worked to understand that she was actually a teammate, a friend, and a learner, in addition to being an athlete. Her speech expanded that idea for all.

Your job or title is not the core of who you are. You are a human doing a job. You might be "doing engineering" right now while you are working on "being" a world-class problem solver. Kelsey encouraged everyone to reframe their thinking from what they are going to *do* to who they are going to *be*.

We now realize that this was how we ended up starting our own company – Lifecycle Insights. Let us rewind just a bit for you.

Prior to Lifecycle Insights, Nick and Marnie started working together in an education technology company more than a decade ago. That company was built around two founders who believed firmly in superior customer support/success and amazing product development. Over an 18-month period, the company was acquired three times. While every acquisition had its challenges, one of them felt like Rupert Mannion (played by Anthony Head) had bought us out.

In the Rupert Mannion version of our company, our customer success team was cut from 17 team members to just 6. The significantly larger sales force oversold the product, debilitating the support team, and halting all development efforts while they worked to stabilize the product. As leaders of the success and support organizations, we spent our days in fire-fighting mode, feeling hopeless about being able to help our customers.

We knew that if we built a company, we would focus on helping our customers be successful by solving their problems with a great product. If you are following our timeline, we did not yet have an idea for a product *nor* did we have a problem to solve. But we had great resolve on how the company would operate.

In a shocking turn of events, we then read a lot of books. ☺ We had never started a software company from scratch before so we read books on business, finance, product development, sales and marketing, customer success, and leadership. We knew how we wanted to run our business in terms of its culture. So between what we had read and what we believed, we developed our core values and fundamental principles by which we would run our business:

◊ **Raving Fans**: We believe in growing Raving Fans with a great customer experience above all.

◊ **Growth**: For everyone. We help our customers scale and grow true partnerships. We help our employees level up and develop skills toward their personal goals.

◊ **Transparency**: We believe that open communication is a critical element to trusted relationships.

◊ **GSD**: We get sh*t done!

◊ **Right people, right seats**: Our focused team consists of independent and innovative thinkers who own a problem and see it to resolution.

◊ **The Three Es**: We aim to Educate through Engagement and Entertainment in the community.

We knew we believed in that whole list of values before we ever ran into a fellow volleyball player of over 20 years who had a business problem to solve and became one of our business partners for the creation of Lifecycle Insights.

We are firm believers that personal and professional core values are the foundational element for success. As we reflect now on our core values, we consider the ingredients required to drive an organization:

◊ Core Values & Culture

◊ Core Values & Decision-Making

◊ Core Values & Diamond Dogs

CORE VALUES & CULTURE

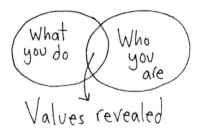

Before Ted learned that his new job as coach of AFC Richmond meant that he was now a "gaffer" on a "pitch" in charge of "training," he knew that the heart of a successful team was creating team culture. To Ted it didn't matter if he was coaching American football or European football, he knew that getting the team believing in Believe and believing in the team were the keys to making it happen.

On the plane to England, he brought along Coach Beard, his never-quit attitude, and an extra helping of his core value – positivity.

This is not an approach that anyone at AFC Richmond saw coming but one that viewers all over the world needed to hear. Comments from the actors' guest appearances on talk shows, podcasts, TikTok reels, blog posts, and Twitter feeds speak to the power of positivity. When people first met Ted, they doubted that power. They saw him as naïve, weak, or gullible... or a clueless Yankee Doodle. But Ted knew the true secret of unlocking a team – and that was by focusing first on each player.

The proof came in Season 1, Episode 3, when Beard asked Ted why he was winding up Roy Kent. Ted answered that if they were going to make a difference, Roy would be the first domino that "needs to fall."

Relentless positivity wasn't Ted's only core value he brought along to the UK. He also packed:

◊ Humility
◊ Teamwork
◊ Resilience

◊   Vulnerability
◊   Continuous improvement

Core values are really the guiding principles of a person, group, or organization. *Culture* represents the way those core values play out day-to-day. *Core values* represent the foundation, and *culture* is the expression of those values in action.

TL;DR[10]

Core values = guiding principles
Culture = the way core values play out

There are a lot of companies that post their core values on their website and their office walls. Their (often former or disgruntled) employees post on social media or job boards that the company culture clashes with those core values. Similarly, many times someone gets hired into a company that is misaligned with their personal values; it doesn't work out because they are not a culture fit.

There was a lot of that clashing in Season 1 of *Ted Lasso*, and it was due to the conflict between the team's existing culture and the one Lasso and Beard were trying to develop. The Lasso and Beard way had not been fully accepted yet. There are plenty of examples that would demonstrate this, but the most entertaining was nearly all of the behavior of Jamie Tartt (do-do-do-do).

Consider Jamie's core values. He started the series focusing on personal success and individual achievement (and his appearance). Jamie played to the crowd and didn't really concern himself with a loss as long as he got credit for his goals and accolades. In all of the research we have done on core values, we have not seen one specifically referencing being a ball-hog, but self-centeredness will cover it nicely.

---

[10] TL;DR = too long; didn't read.

Clearly Jamie's core values got in the way of "that team building we are trying to do here." It was evident what that did to the culture of the team.

◊ Jamie laughed as Colin and Isaac bullied Nate.

◊ He made fun of Sam Obisanya when Sam didn't play well.

◊ He constantly mocked Roy Kent for losing his star power on the pitch.

All of these behaviors led to a divided locker room, which had a nightmare effect on the field.

That is how core values and culture play out. Core values are the beliefs that guide your behaviors, and culture is what it looks and feels like. If the two are out of alignment, no organization or group (or kids in the backseat of a car) will get along.

Core values are the beliefs that guide your behaviors.

Viewers delighted in watching Ted, Roy, and Keeley help Jamie go through the growing pains of becoming a better version of himself. From self-centered to team-oriented and growth-focused, Jamie won the hearts of many as he developed humility and a sense of team.

In the realm of business success, core values and culture stand as pillars that underpin an organization's every move. The book *The Culture Code* by Daniel Coyle delves into the essence of building a cohesive and thriving culture. At its core, defining the core values that guide a company's behavior is akin to setting a moral compass for the organization. These guiding principles act as a North star, providing direction and a shared sense of purpose for every member of the team.

Fostering a culture that aligns with these core values is where the true magic happens. In *The Culture Code*, Coyle highlights how groups like the U.S. Navy SEALs cultivate an ethos of trust, collaboration, and accountability. This aligns with the idea of instilling a culture that resonates with established core values.

When values are not just words on a page but ingrained in the DNA of an organization, they form the basis for a cohesive and high-performing team. The SEALs' success stems from an unwavering dedication to their core values, which permeates every aspect of their operations.

In recent years, there has been a noticeable shift in the way organizations approach leadership and management. Traditional Human Resources departments, which were primarily focused on administrative tasks such as recruitment, benefits administration, and compliance, have evolved into more dynamic and strategic entities known as People and Culture organizations. This transformation represents a fundamental change in the way companies view their employees – not merely as resources, but as integral contributors to the organization's success.

Culture is how those core values look and feel in everyday life.

One of the critical elements that will be discussed later is the need for communication around your core values in order to help to create your culture. From hiring practices to onboarding to team-building activities and monthly/weekly/daily meetings, the company needs to live and breathe those core values.

The Great Resignation, quiet quitting, and other economic factors spurred on by the pandemic have highlighted concerns for employees and the desire to align their personal values with the values and culture of the company they work for. No longer are all employees signing up with the intent to stay in an organization for the next 30 years. Instead, they are looking for self-improvement and growth as individuals. Companies that do well to accurately reflect their core values and live them in their culture will be best positioned to hire right-fit candidates who have compatible personal values.

In Part Four, we will walk through some activities to help you define your personal core values. There is no Roy Kent head-butting or three-a-day runs for this part of the training, but it is good to take a look at who you are and who you want to be.

CORE VALUES & DECISION-MAKING

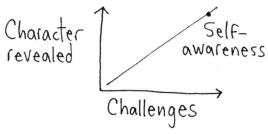

Utilizing core values as filters in decision-making ensures that choices align with an organization's guiding principles. This approach enhances integrity, builds trust, and contributes to a culture where values are upheld in all aspects of the organization's operations.

Crucially, the reflection of these values in every decision and action is paramount. It's not enough for core values to be mere statements; they must be living, breathing guides to every choice made within the organization. The importance of this is vividly portrayed in *The Culture Code* as it details the San Antonio Spurs, an NBA team renowned for its consistent success. Their adherence to values like teamwork, selflessness, and discipline isn't confined to the basketball court; it is evident in the meticulous planning of strategies, the support extended to team members, and even in the recruitment process.

The intersection of core values and culture serves as a testament to the transformative power of these principles in driving business success. By setting clear values that resonate with the organization's purpose, fostering a culture that embodies these values, and ensuring that they permeate every decision and action, businesses can lay the foundation for sustained growth and excellence. In the cases of the SEALs and the Spurs, these principles have propelled them to extraordinary heights, reinforcing the notion that a well-defined culture anchored in core values is not just a competitive advantage, but the bedrock of enduring success.

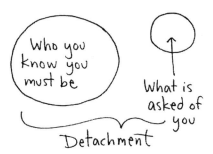

Excuse us for a second, while we get on our soapbox. In this age of technology, there is no shortage of data and information to help guide decisions. That said, because of the overwhelming amount of information, people don't ask the right questions of the information and get bad answers – a lot like Rupert Mannion, who was pretty confident that Ted was going to miss the target in a game of darts. (Barbecue Sauce ☺).

That is actually a great analogy. The data and information that we have should help us hit our target. But people are not using it the right way. We see this a lot in folks who are looking for their first job and have applied to our company. Using a popular job post app, we launched a very specific listing which included a discussion of our core values, as well as the requirement to send a video answering three questions (including the answer to whether or not the applicant believes that a hotdog is a sandwich).

Within seconds we had automated applications in our inbox. There were 37 of them. Within three days we had 234 applicants. We read through about 60 of them and stopped. In our email, we found only five videos from folks who had actually read the job posting and believed they would be a good fit for our company. Most important (yes, we mean that), they all had opinions on hot dogs and sandwiches.

To the 229 folks who did not land interviews (or frankly much more than a glance) for our job, there are some lessons to be learned on the football pitch. Getting a job is a lot like scoring a goal. You may have to take multiple shots but the smartest players wait to take the *right* shots. Football/soccer games (as Ted now knows) have two halves equaling 90 minutes of play. There are thousands of passes (pieces of information), maybe dozens of goal attempts, often resulting in less than a handful of successful outcomes.

You need to take the same approach in your decision-making. Find the right shots to take.

How do you do that? By reviewing the data and aligning that information with your core values to make the decision. It was very clear that, of the 234 folks who applied for our job, the vast majority did not do that work.

Penalty Kick: The failed applicants relied on automation to do all the work for them. Remember that all automation is not *good* automation.

In collaborating with high school and college students (and really anyone in the job market), we have found that they often know a good bit about job titles and career options, since that is their vision or goal. Where these young people struggle, or sometimes miss altogether, is understanding their own core values and then aligning their decisions with those values.

Many companies post their core values online. Goodness knows all of the company review sites like Glassdoor and Indeed have no shortage of current and former employees providing insights into whether or not the culture actually aligns with those values. Great questions to ask in interviews are around not just the entity's core values but what that looks like in day-to-day operations and decisions.

Time Out: If you hear bells and whistles (or Roy yelling, "Whistle! Whistle!") because you needed to hear this, we will help you work through some activities in The Game section.

CORE VALUES & DIAMOND DOGS

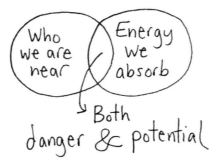

Both
danger & potential

Diamond Dogs exist to hold you accountable to your own personal core values.

One of Marnie's former students recently tried to commit suicide. Thankfully, he was unsuccessful. Also thankfully, he is glad he was unsuccessful. Since that time, the two of them have had a lot of conversations around mental health and the support he needs in his life.

One of the conversations centered around the notion of having your own Diamond Dogs. We all remember fondly the day that Roy Kent finally asked to become a Diamond Dog. He was looking for people he trusted to listen, to give a variety of viewpoints, and to support him in what he needed.

As Marnie drove her former student to one of his many doctors' follow-ups, they often discussed the crowd that he hung around. He knew that some of them weren't the best influences or particularly supportive of him trying to "level up" as he said. She brought up the popular notion that we are the average of the five folks we spend the most time with. So she asked who those five folks were for him. Then she asked which ones brought value to his world and which ones dragged him down. In the course of the conversation, he actually decided for himself that maybe he needed to "relegate" some of those friends out of the top five. He knew that he needed a support team, and that he needed to include his new AA counselor in his group of Diamond Dogs. (We have no idea what the counselor looks like, but we're picturing Dr. Sharon.)

As of the writing of this book, Marnie's former student goes to his counseling sessions three days a week while holding down a job. He has even been asked to consider becoming a counselor himself. He is glad to share any of the details of the story in hopes that it will help someone else take the steps they need toward better mental health.

Penalty Kick: It's important to remember that *Ted Lasso* was a television show and so timelines don't necessarily match the way things work in the real world. As a therapist, Dr. Sharon Fieldstone would certainly tell anyone that therapy is not a one-time magic bullet. It takes work. In the show, it played well for quick realization of the benefits of getting mental health help, but if that is something you as a reader or viewer struggle with, know that therapy too requires work. But the work is 100% worth it. We are rooting for you!

Now let's talk about how Diamond Dogs can help support you to live up to your core values.

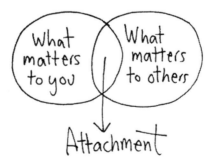

The Diamond Dogs were more than just support for Ted as head gaffer of AFC Richmond. They were his trusted advisors, support system, and accountabilibuddies. They weren't just invested in the success of the team but also the success and growth of each of the Diamond Dogs as human beings. The first name Ted suggested for the group was the "EQ Warriors" – EQ, meaning Emotional

Quotient, showing that this group was formed to support each other emotionally.

There are lots of writings on the topic that "it is lonely at the top." The leader is often siloed from everyone else in an organization because everyone else reports to them. This puts the leader on a pedestal that makes them feel as though they cannot show weakness (mental, physical, or emotional). That is why everyone needs their own Diamond Dogs.

While Ted's Diamond Dogs were all part of AFC Richmond, most people find their support systems in different areas of their lives. It is much less important what job they do, than who they are for you. One important call out is that just because you have a group of friends does not mean they are necessarily your Diamond Dogs.

Here are the key elements of your Diamond Dogs:

◊ **Accountability**: Each member is responsible for their actions and their impact on the group. The group holds each other accountable to living by their core values.

◊ **Empathy**: They actively listen and understand each others' perspectives, fostering a sense of unity.

◊ **Trust**: They have confidence in each others' abilities and intentions. They can be open and vulnerable, confiding in each other because they create a safe space.

◊ **Communication**: They maintain open and honest dialogue, ensuring everyone is informed and aligned.

◊ **Respect**: They treat each other with dignity, valuing their unique contributions.

If you were to ask yourself one question to determine if someone is your Diamond Dog, answer this question:

Would you pick up a phone call from them at 3:00 AM?

Then ask yourself:

> *Are you the kind of person that they would accept a 3:00 AM call from?*

These are your greatest fans and the bond you have created allows them also to be your biggest critics. As you strive to become the best version of yourself, these are your people who will hold you accountable to your core values and help get you there.

In the next section, we will set our sights on Vision and Purpose to chart a path to where you are going.

Interested in more readings on Core Values and Culture?
Check out what might be on Beard's bookshelf...

• *Leading with the Heart*, Mike Krzyzewski and Donald T. Phillips

• *Culture Code*, Daniel Coyle

• *The Advantage*, Patrick Lencioni

• *Drive*, Daniel Pink

• *Daring Greatly*, Brené Brown

5 VISION & PURPOSE

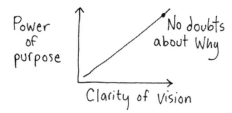

Vision and *purpose* are the twin engines (two aces, like Jamie and Dani!) that drive meaningful leadership. A *vision* is a vivid mental picture of a desirable future state, a beacon that leads individuals or organizations toward a higher aspiration. It provides direction, clarity, and a rallying point for all endeavors. *Purpose,* on the other hand, is the profound sense of why, the underlying reason that fuels actions with meaning and significance. It fills every task, decision, and effort with a deeper understanding of the greater impact.

TL;DR

Vision = mental picture of the desired future

Purpose = your why

Ted Lasso's arrival at AFC Richmond wasn't just a coaching change; it was the spark of a transformative vision. Now, Rebecca's vision wasn't aligned at the start, but Ted got her there. His unwavering belief in the potential of the team, and the power of positivity, set the stage for a remarkable journey. Much to the shock of reporters – especially Trent Crimm – Ted didn't focus on wins and losses. Beyond victories on the field, Ted's vision extended to creating a culture of inclusivity, personal growth, and camaraderie. This broader vision shaped not only the team's performance but also the players' lives beyond the game.

Every successful leader has a guiding purpose that transcends day-to-day tasks. Ted's purpose was clear: "It is not about the wins and losses, it is about helping these young men become the best versions of themselves." This is why he always worked to inspire and uplift everyone he encountered, both on and off the field. Ted's actions consistently aligned with his purpose. Whether it was motivating a struggling player or fostering a sense of belonging within the team, every move reflected his deeply ingrained purpose.

It was clear that Ted and Coach Beard knew a lot of books, songs, and kitschy phrases. In all of their discussions, they rarely referenced specific leadership styles (outside of John Wooden's Pyramid of Success). That said, they were shining examples of modern leadership both as transformational leaders and servant leaders. Modern transformative leadership, at its core, emphasizes continuous learning, adaptability, and collaboration. In addition, the dynamic duo embodied servant leadership, a philosophy that prioritizes the well-being and growth of team members.

A vision is a beacon that leads individuals or organizations toward higher aspirations.

In the landscape of modern leadership, qualities such as adaptability, empathy, and a focus on the growth and well-being of team members have become paramount. Ted Lasso and Coach Beard epitomize these principles, showcasing how transformational and servant leadership can drive success in today's complex and ever-evolving business world. If Ted and Coach Beard had run a board room instead of a locker room, they might have handed out some of these books by some renowned experts.

For Rebecca: Simon Sinek, the celebrated author of *Start with Why*, firmly asserts that vision is rooted in understanding the fundamental reasons behind our actions. He contends that genuine leaders delve deep into the "why" of their endeavors, recognizing that this intrinsic understanding propels not only themselves but their teams toward meaningful objectives. Sinek's philosophy underscores the notion that a compelling "why" forms the cornerstone of any enduring vision.

For Higgins: Jim Collins, in his seminal work *Good to Great*, underscores the importance of assembling the right team. He maintains that visionary leaders excel at discerning the individuals who not only share their passion but are also adeptly positioned to contribute to the collective journey. By ensuring that each team member occupies a role that aligns with their strengths and aspirations, leaders set the stage for the seamless execution of the shared vision. Collins's insight highlights that vision isn't solely about a grand idea but also about the people who bring it to life. He is frequently quoted as identifying the need to put the right people in the right seats.

For Nate: Dan Sullivan, founder of Strategic Coach, introduces the concept of a "Unique Ability" as an indispensable element of one's sense of purpose. In his view, understanding what makes us exceptional allows us to tap into our fullest potential. This resonates with the idea that a clear sense of purpose not only guides our personal development but also enables us to make distinctive contributions within a team or organization. Sullivan's perspective serves as a potent reminder that within each person lies a unique strength that can be harnessed to drive the collective vision forward.

> *Purpose is the underlying reason that fuels actions with meaning and significance.*

The synergy between vision and purpose creates a powerful force in leadership. A clear vision provides the framework, setting the course for action. Purpose, in turn, fuels the engine, driving each step with passion, commitment, and authenticity. This combo-platter ignites a transformative journey toward realizing goals, even in the face of adversity.

In the realm of servant leadership, defining core principles is paramount. For Ted, this translates into an unwavering commitment to positivity and solutions. Ted's business operating system revolves around maintaining a relentlessly positive outlook, even in the face of challenges. This principle not only guides his actions but also sets the tone for the entire team, fostering a culture of resilience and forward-thinking problem solving. Through his mission to inspire belief and courage, Ted embodies the essence of creating a business operating system rooted in optimism and solution-oriented thinking.

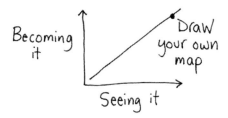

Embracing a clear vision and a defined purpose isn't just a leadership trait – it's a transformative force that can shape teams, organizations, and even entire communities. Ted Lasso's impact wasn't confined to the soccer pitch. His influence extended into the personal lives of his players and the broader community, exemplifying the potential of visionary leadership in any context.

In our quest to Lead It Like Lasso, let's remember that vision and purpose are the stars we steer by on the path to excellence.

There are three components that any business or individual needs to focus on defining their operating system:

◇ Vision
◇ Purpose
◇ Goals

VISION

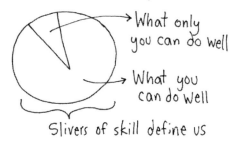

In The Rules chapter, we talked about the elements that help to define your personal operating system. Now we are going to start to take a look at what goals you have for your organization or yourself – your vision.

If your core values are the "how," your vision is the "what" you want to accomplish. Successful organizations make sure that they have a very clear vision statement, as this is the foundation for all of their decisions and actions moving forward.

Here are a couple examples of successful vision statements:

◊ **Google**: To provide access to the world's information in one click.

◊ **Tesla**: To create the most compelling car company of the 21st century by driving the world's transition to electric vehicles.

◊ **Starbucks**: To inspire and nurture the human spirit – one person, one cup, and one neighborhood at a time.

Vision statements are not just for businesses. Individuals also have visions for their futures:

◊ To save enough money for retirement for a second home at the lake.

◊ To have a job I enjoy so that I can do the things I love.

◊ To be successful so I can expand my world through travel.

◊   To get healthier so I can be an active participant in my grandchildren's lives.

A vision statement is there to set guide rails for how you go about accomplishing your goals. There are lots of business books around vision. Shout out to some of our favorite authors on the topic: Jim Collins's *Good to Great*, Eric Ries's *The Lean Startup*, and Gino Wickman's *Traction*.

Recently we participated in a vision-setting activity with our friend and CEO of Result Maps, Scott Levy. Scott has done this workshop for Fortune 100 companies and startups alike. (FYI, in The Game section, Scott has given us permission to share his vision-setting activity so that you can work through this for your business, and we have adapted it to our own framework of a personal operating system at **LeadItLikeLasso.com**.)

As we worked through the activity, some key elements we took away were:

◊   Clarity of vision is critical in order for everyone to aim for the same target.

◊   That clarity provides guide rails (or bowling bumper pads) to help reduce decision fatigue and ensure alignment.

◊   By starting out with a big picture of what success looks like for you, and zooming in repeatedly, you build a system of strategy and tactics that support your vision.

Start by painting a very clear picture of your goals for three years out. Imagine what will be different by then. The more detail you have, the better your guide rails will be. Because of that vision, what does that mean? What will you need to do within the next quarter? What actions will you take toward those goals to help hit those objectives? Then what does that mean you should focus on this week?

In Scott's vision-setting workshop he talked about a company vision behaving like bumper pads in bowling. Any errant behaviors or actions will bump along those rails and get funneled back closer to the target.

We think a lot about how parenting is a leadership role. A common vision parents have for their children is that they will grow up healthy and happy. Because most children don't know how to make choices in line with that vision, parents are there to guide them.

We recognize in our own lives that parenting often comes off as nagging.

◊ "Get off the screens."

◊ "Go get some exercise."

◊ "No cookies before dinner."

We've all been there.

It's hard enough to support that vision when you are cooking every meal for your children, but it is even harder at picnics, parties, and other gatherings, where supervision and access to snacks are dramatically different than in your kitchen.

Trick Play: Marnie came up with this lifehack Party Rule.

> *"If you want a snack, you do not have to ask*
> *as long as you have seven fruits*
> *or vegetables before you eat it."*

It really was that simple. This party rule gave her kids some autonomy to be able to decide that they could have a snack, and it helped them understand that the reason they couldn't have six snacks is because it wasn't helping them be healthy and that it was important to balance what is good for you with what might taste good. Plus, it felt a lot less like nagging/micromanaging.

More than once, Marnie saw seven carrots, exactly seven, land on her son's plate next to a brownie. Was this a perfect system? No, but it certainly kept down on nagging at parties and made a bigger impact than she suspected. Twenty years later, her adult friends mock her by walking out with seven carrots in their hands, saying, "Okay Miss Marnie, I'm going to get a brownie after I eat these."

As companies grow or as kids grow up, strategies may change, but the vision really doesn't. Think about all of the changes and strategies that AFC Richmond implemented over the course of three seasons. Dani Rojas came to the team and they had to figure out how to work with two aces. Then one ace and two kings when Zava (Maximilian Osinski) arrived. One Zava – then everyone else. That created an entirely different ecosystem. Roy suggested the traditional 4-4-2 system[11] that "they had been playing since they were fucking kids." Then in a moment of clarity later that season, Jamie explained to the locker room that they should "not play *to* me but play *through* me." Throughout all of this, the ultimate vision never changed (because great teams do great things), and AFC Richmond eventually found the right strategy.

PURPOSE

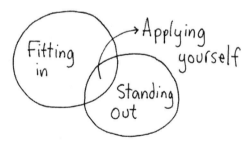

Any vision without a purpose is just a directive. That would be the "Because I said so" approach to leading or parenting. Having a purpose answers the big "why" for an organization.

---

[11] "4-4-2" is a common soccer formation where the team starts four defenders, four midfielders and two strikers.

Let's take a look at the whys for the businesses we mentioned earlier:

◊ Google's founders, Larry Page and Sergey Brin, believed that information should be easily accessible and organized for everyone. Their vision was driven by a desire to democratize information, making it universally available and useful.

◊ Tesla's CEO, Elon Musk, is passionate about reducing humanity's dependence on fossil fuels and combating climate change. His vision is rooted in a desire to revolutionize transportation and accelerate the shift toward sustainable energy sources.

◊ Starbucks founder, Howard Schultz, wanted to create a place where people could connect, find a sense of belonging, and enjoy high-quality coffee. His vision was motivated by a belief in the power of community and the importance of human connection.

These companies' vision statements are deeply aligned with the personal beliefs and values of their founders, reflecting a larger purpose beyond just profitability. Each statement reflects a clear intention to make a positive impact on the world in a way that is meaningful to them.

There is a popular activity that companies often do to find their purpose. It is to ask "5 Whys"[12] around your vision.

Let's take a look at how this technique would play out for AFC Richmond.

---

[12] Sakichi Toyoda, the Japanese industrialist, inventor, and founder of Toyota Industries, developed the "5 Whys" technique in the 1930s. It became popular in the 1970s, and Toyota still uses it to solve problems today.

At the very core of Ted's vision was the notion of team building that, done right, would grow a successful club. To get to his purpose, ask "5 whys."

Why would he do this?

—*Because a team that supports each other can win.*

Why?

—*Because teams that play together stay together.*

Why?

—*Because they trust each other to make the right decisions on and off the field for the team.*

Why?

—*Because they know they have done the work.*

Why?

—*Because this helps everyone level up to become a better version of themselves.*

SMART GOALS

Ted had a vision of creating a cohesive team to help level up each of the players with a goal of "winning the whole f'ing thing!" Ted showed how those components could play out on a comedic football pitch.

Once AFC Richmond – or any organization, from Fortune 500 companies to school districts and Boy Scout troops – has a vision and purpose, the groundwork has been done to accomplish their goals.

The more clarity there is around a goal, the easier it is to align the humans and work to make it happen. The most popular method for writing clear goals is to ensure they are SMART goals – specific, measurable, attainable, realistic, and timebound.

While "winning the whole f'ing thing" was pretty clear in the context of *Ted Lasso*, let's take a more formal look at it.

Specific	Win the Premier League Title
Measurable	Earn the most points (ranking)
Attainable	Darn tootin' it's attainable – we're 1 of 20 clubs!
Realistic	Well, some would have argued, but not Ted. And not the team. They *believed*.
Timebound	Season 3.

As we will see in the section on Growth, the "SMART"er your goals are, the easier it will be to clearly define and communicate the strategies to succeed.

Let's take a look at a couple of real-life examples of vision, purpose, and their aligned goals.

Business: APPLE INC.

Apple Inc., under the visionary leadership of Steve Jobs, offered a compelling example of how a robust business operating system can transform an organization and an industry. Jobs's unwavering commitment to innovation and user-centric design became the cornerstone of Apple's success.

Steve Jobs believed in simplicity, elegance, and putting the customer experience above all else. He famously said, "Design is not just what it looks like and feels like. Design is how it works." This principle guided Apple's product development, from the intuitive user interfaces to the sleek hardware design. Apple's mission to "bring the best user experience to its customers through its innovative hardware, software, and services" was more than just a statement – it was a guiding philosophy. This clarity of purpose directed every aspect of the company's operations, from product development to marketing.

Apple's product launches were meticulously planned, with specific goals in mind. Whether it was the launch of the iPhone, iPad, or other groundbreaking products, Apple set precise targets for sales, market share, and customer satisfaction. These goals were not only specific and measurable but also achievable and relevant to the broader vision.

Sports: MANCHESTER CITY FOOTBALL CLUB

Under the management of Pep Guardiola, Manchester City exemplified the power of a well-defined operating system in the world of sports. Guardiola's philosophy, known as "tiki-taka," places emphasis on possession-based football with rapid passing and movement. This system not only defines how the team plays on the field but also shapes recruitment decisions, training routines, and player development strategies.

Guardiola's core principles of possession, movement, and teamwork are evident in every aspect of the club's operations. The mission to play attractive, attacking football is mirrored in the club's style of play, which consistently aims to entertain fans while achieving success on the field. The SMART goals set by the club include targets for league positions, cup runs, and performance metrics for individual players – all aligned with the overarching vision of playing attractive, successful football.

As Jim Collins would say, now that the vision is clear, the most critical element is ensuring that the right people are in the right seats to make it happen.

Led Tasso... *a counter-example*

In Season 2, Episode 3, Ted Lasso storms out of his office as his alter-ego "Led Tasso," a perfect counter-example of Ted's normal coaching style. Instead of positive and collaborative, Led Tasso is mean, dictatorial, and unyielding.

In this scene, Led Tasso employs a clever tactic to unite the team and encourage Jamie Tartt's participation... a comically exaggerated version of himself, using reverse psychology to motivate the players. By temporarily adopting this persona, Ted prompts the team to band together, setting aside their distrust of Jamie's return and focusing on their shared goal. This unexpected approach ultimately proves effective, leading to a stronger sense of camaraderie among the players, and creating an opportunity for Jamie to contribute to the team's success.

In a TV series, this plays perfectly. It also demonstrates how the opposite of what Ted Lasso is actually trying to achieve would be an unbearable situation. In that light, a counter-example of what *not* to do is often an effective learning tool. So let's take a look at a real-world example of a company that did not have a clear vision and purpose.

One notable example of a company that faced challenges due to a lack of clear vision and purpose is Sears, once a retail giant in the United States. Sears, Roebuck and Co. was founded in the late 19th century and became a dominant force in the retail industry. However, as the retail landscape evolved and shifted to e-commerce and specialty stores, Sears struggled to define its identity and adapt to changing consumer preferences.

The company faced issues with outdated stores, ineffective marketing strategies, and a failure to differentiate itself from competitors. The lack of a cohesive and forward-thinking vision hindered Sears's ability to pivot and compete effectively in the rapidly evolving retail market. This ultimately led to financial difficulties, including bankruptcy in 2018.

Sears's decline serves as a cautionary tale about the importance of having a clear vision and purpose to guide a company through changing times and remain relevant in a dynamic business environment.

Interested in more readings on Vision and Purpose?
Check out what might be on Beard's bookshelf...

- *You Win in the Locker Room First*, Jon Gordon and Mike Smith

- *Start with Why,* Simon Sinek

- *Leaders Eat Last*, Simon Sinek

- *Good to Great*, James C. Collins

- *Who Not How,* Dan Sullivan

6 COMMUNICATION

& INFLUENCE

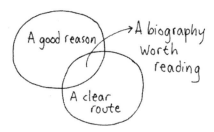

Core values and culture... Check ✓.

Vision and purpose... Check ✓.

We are feeling pretty good about ourselves at this point. No matter what leadership position we are in, we have identified our core values, and we have a good idea of the type of culture we want to live and work in. Beyond that, we have an established vision and have the "why" or purpose supporting that vision.

Now we need to focus on the foundational elements that will support our core values, culture, vision, and purpose. One of the central components that will act as the foundation to execute on any vision is a comprehensive and effective communication strategy.

In this section, we highlight real-world examples of effective communication strategies that were critical in executing leadership vision. We of course will also cite examples of how Ted Lasso demonstrated similar strategies to propel AFC Richmond from a struggling football club to one of the more successful teams in the league at the end of Season 3.

As Ted might say, *"Communication is a lot like wrestling a marshmallow. It's hard to wrap your hands around the details, and things can get sticky."*

Communication impacts every element in an organization or family. We will take a look at the following keys to communication:

◊ Emotional Intelligence (EQ)
◊ Stakeholder Engagement
◊ Influencing Skills
◊ Teamwork

EMOTIONAL INTELLIGENCE (EQ)

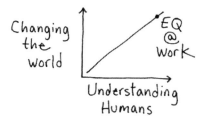

The unofficial Season 1 poll of Ted Lasso's performance from AFC Richmond's fanbase was not pretty. It looked something like:

Wanker: 99%
Let's wait and see: 1%.

It was clear that Ted didn't know a thing about football and even less about the way of life in England. The entire community questioned his Intelligence Quotient (IQ). What we quickly realized however was that Ted rated extremely high in terms of Emotional Intelligence (EQ). So much so, that his EQ traits represent a big reason why we wrote this book!

EQ refers to a person's ability to recognize, understand, and effectively utilize their own emotions and those of others in various social and interpersonal situations. It encompasses a range of skills, including self-awareness, self-regulation, empathy, and social skills. EQ is crucial in communication because it shapes how individuals perceive, interpret, and respond to both verbal and nonverbal cues from others.

In communication, individuals with high EQ are better equipped to engage in empathetic listening, accurately interpret the emotional nuances of a conversation, and tailor their responses to the emotional needs of their audience. They can navigate difficult conversations with greater ease, remain calm under pressure, and build rapport by conveying genuine understanding and consideration.

Do you remember Ted's press conference when Trent Crimm (*The Independent*) asked how Dani was doing after Earl the greyhound mascot died. It was a difficult convo he navigated with ease, while remaining calm and conveying genuine understanding and consideration. *EQ!*

In contrast, individuals with lower EQ may struggle with emotional triggers, misinterpretation of others' emotions, and ineffective responses – leading to misunderstandings, conflicts, and breakdowns in communication. Therefore, EQ significantly impacts the quality and effectiveness of interpersonal communication, contributing to better relationships and successful interactions in both personal and professional settings.

In his groundbreaking book *Emotional Intelligence: Why It Can Matter More Than IQ,* Daniel Goleman explores the concept of EQ and its significance in personal and professional success. Goleman argues that EQ can be even more critical than traditional intelligence, IQ, in determining a person's ability to thrive in various aspects of life.

His book delves into the idea that EQ can be cultivated and improved over time, offering practical techniques to enhance one's emotional intelligence. Goleman presents compelling research and real-life examples to illustrate how individuals with higher EQ are often better equipped to handle stress, build strong relationships, and excel in leadership roles. This is especially true in roles that involve human interaction and engagement. He emphasizes the importance of recognizing and managing one's emotions, as well as understanding and relating to the emotions of others, as key elements of emotional intelligence.

Are you picking up what we are putting down? Ted's high EQ is one of the key drivers that allows him to be an effective leader. The traits of high-EQ individuals have a direct correlation to effective communication and influence.

Yes, individuals can improve their emotional intelligence (EQ) through conscious effort and practice. Here are some specific ways to enhance EQ:

1) Self-Awareness

Practice self-reflection: Regularly take time to assess your emotions, triggers, and reactions.

Keep a journal: Write down your feelings and thoughts to gain insight into your emotional patterns.

Seek feedback: Ask trusted friends, family members, or colleagues for honest feedback ("Oklahoma!"[13]) about your behavior and how it affects others.

2) Self-Regulation

Develop stress management techniques: Learn techniques like deep breathing, meditation, or exercise to manage stress and emotional reactions.

---

[13] A codeword suggested by Ted and his wife Michelle's marital counselor that they could use when they wanted their partner to answer with "the God's honest truth."

Pause and think: When faced with strong emotions, take a moment to pause and consider your response before reacting impulsively.

3) **Empathy**

Practice active listening: Pay full attention to others when they speak, and try to understand their perspective.

Engage in diverse interactions: Interact with people from different backgrounds and perspectives to broaden your understanding of human emotions and experiences.

Ask open-ended questions: Encourage others to share their thoughts and feelings by asking questions that invite discussion.

4) **Social Skills**

Improve communication: Work on your verbal and nonverbal communication skills to convey empathy and understanding.

Resolve conflicts: Learn conflict resolution techniques, such as active listening and compromise.

Build relationships: Actively nurture and maintain positive relationships by showing appreciation and support.

5) **Emotional Management**

Identify and name emotions: Develop a vocabulary to describe your emotions accurately.

Learn to express emotions: Express your feelings in a healthy and constructive manner rather than suppressing or exploding with them.

6) **Continuous Learning**

Read and educate yourself: Books, articles, and workshops on emotional intelligence can provide valuable insights and strategies.

Seek coaching or therapy: Professional guidance can help you work through specific emotional challenges and develop your EQ.

7) Practice Compassion

Engage in acts of kindness: Volunteering or helping others can enhance your sense of empathy and compassion.

Build genuine relationships: Focus on forming meaningful connections with people rather than superficial interactions.

Practice perspective-taking: Try to understand others' viewpoints and feelings even when you disagree.

Remember that improving EQ is an ongoing process. It takes time and effort, but the benefits in personal and professional relationships, as well as overall wellbeing, can be significant in terms of how we communicate with others. Start by identifying which aspects of EQ you'd like to enhance and gradually incorporate these practices into your daily life.

STAKEHOLDER ENGAGEMENT

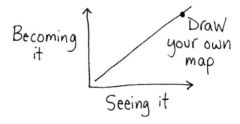

Developing a higher EQ is a foundational component of your communication strategy, especially helpful with one-to-one interactions. That being said, we need to also consider a broader context with an effective communication strategy. Specifically, we need to consider each of our stakeholders, and if/how our communication strategy may be different for each group.

Consider Ted Lasso's stakeholders for a moment. Ted had a number of them in the show, including his players, his coaching staff, the team owner, the media, and of course the rabid fanbase of AFC Richmond supporters.

There are certainly common threads with how Ted interacted with each of these stakeholders. The most obvious was that Ted always demonstrated high EQ when interacting with anyone on an individual level. He showed empathy and compassion, was always self-aware of his own emotions, and also took into account the emotions of the person he was interacting with.

Another common thread across all Ted's communication with his stakeholders was the way he remained in alignment with his vision and purpose. "Believe" and "becoming the best version of yourself" stayed consistent in all of Ted's communication with these parties.

"Believe" communication examples by stakeholder groups.

Stakeholder	
Players	Ted hangs a Believe sign in the locker room and has countless team meetings asking the team to believe. "You say 'impossible.' All I see is 'I'm Possible'."
Coaching Staff	Ted values the input and ideas of Nate Shelley, the kit man who aspires to be more involved in coaching. Despite Nate's initial lack of confidence, Ted believes in his potential and starts involving Nate in team discussions and training sessions, giving him the opportunity to grow.
Ownership	Ted asks Rebecca to believe in his unorthodox approach and that the team can be so much more than a notion of revenge against Rupert.
Media	In a press conference, a reporter off-handedly comments: "Can you imagine?" Ted replies, "Yes, because I am right-brain dominant with a strength in make-believe." (A different kind of believe... but he believes in Believe!)
AFC Richmond Supporters	Open practices that the fans can attend, helping them come to Believe.

"SAME BUT DIFFERENT"

A well thought out vision and purpose, along with core values, will allow you to be consistent throughout your communication strategies across stakeholder groups. Indeed, they should form the basis for all of your communication.

This was certainly true with Ted Lasso, however, even with the fictional story of AFC Richmond, it does become apparent that a comprehensive communication strategy should allow for variation across different stakeholder groups.

Consider Ted's general approach to interacting with the media versus his players. His press conferences were often presented with vulnerability, and at times it was awkward to watch (and you couldn't help but feel sympathy for him — or root for him). In contrast, most of his interactions with the players were presented with confidence. While the approaches were vastly different, the message remained the same. Specifically, we believe we are doing the right things to be the best version of ourselves, and when that happens, results will follow.

The magic of Ted Lasso is that through his communication strategy, he ended up aligning the interests of all stakeholders with his overall vision. Yes, each stakeholder was won over and their belief got them pulling in the same direction. Even the crowd at Mae's bar bought in. Powerful!

This does not just happen on TV. When an effective communication strategy is crafted in the real world, the results can be just as successful!

Business: PATAGONIA

Patagonia is an American outdoor clothing and gear company that specializes in products designed for outdoor and recreational activities. The company's business revolves around providing high-quality, sustainable, and environmentally-conscious apparel and gear for individuals who engage in activities such as hiking, camping, climbing, skiing, surfing, and other outdoor pursuits. Their products are comfortable and not too bulky. They keep us warm when it's freezing outside, and they keep us dry when it's wet. Maybe Ted and his coaching staff at AFC Richmond should stock up on some Patagonia gear for the winter-months!

Besides making great outdoor and recreational gear, Patagonia also represents excellence in stakeholder engagement. Patagonia is renowned for its commitment to environmental and social responsibility. The company has consistently demonstrated excellence in stakeholder engagement by prioritizing the needs and concerns of various stakeholders, including employees, customers, suppliers, environmental organizations, and the broader community. (That's a lot of stakeholders to consider!)

Let's take a look at some practices of Patagonia, and how they have addressed the various stakeholders:

1. **Environmental Initiatives**: Patagonia has been a leader in sustainable business practices. They are known for their commitment to reducing their environmental footprint. The company has taken numerous steps to minimize its impact on the environment, such as using organic and recycled materials in their products, reducing water and energy consumption in their supply chain, and advocating for policies to combat climate change.

2. **Supply Chain Transparency**: Patagonia has actively engaged with its suppliers to improve labor conditions, ethical sourcing, and transparency. They have implemented the Fair Trade Certification program for some of their products, ensuring fair wages and safe working conditions for the people who make their clothes.

3. **Customer Engagement**: Patagonia has cultivated a loyal customer base by aligning its products with its environmental values. They have encouraged customers to buy only what they need and to repair their gear rather than replace it. This commitment

to longevity and sustainability has resonated with consumers who share similar values.

4. **Activism and Advocacy**: The company's leadership has not shied away from taking public stances on environmental and social issues. They have used their platform to advocate for the protection of public lands, the reduction of single-use plastics, and other causes aligned with their mission. In 2016, they even pledged to donate 100% of Black Friday sales to grassroots environmental organizations.

5. **Employee Wellbeing**: Patagonia has created a company culture that values work-life balance, wellness, and personal growth. They offer unique benefits, such as paid time off for activism, and have consistently been recognized as a great place to work.

Patagonia's leadership has demonstrated that a company can be successful while simultaneously addressing the concerns and values of various stakeholders. We would argue that not only have they proved they can be successful, but by identifying and then engaging with these stakeholders, Patagonia has thrived. Their commitment to environmental and social responsibility has not only earned them a dedicated customer base but has also set a standard for how companies can engage with stakeholders in a meaningful and responsible way.

We will admit that developing a communication strategy appears easy when done right. It is of course not always easy and you feel it when done wrong.

Penalty Kick: Being a parent is hard!

When looking at leadership and communication, there is no greater challenge than raising children. Many parents (including us) view youth sports as a way for our children to learn several life lessons. Many of them are covered in this book, but we wanted to share a story about when parental communication was not aligned between stakeholders.

If you've been to a youth match, you have probably seen and heard it – the parent is rooting for their child (loudly) and when adversity hits, you hear the parent say, "Suck it up," "Work through it," "No pain no gain," or something else in a

When looking at leadership and communication, there is no greater challenge than raising children.

similar fashion. Not ten minutes later, the referee makes a questionable call, and that same parent yells an obscenity or not-nice thing at the referee.

This is an example of how spoken core values can clash with actual culture.

How does this play out? Yup, through communication. Is anyone surprised when this child, whose parent tried to impress upon him/her to work through resiliency, in turn yells at a teammate for making a bad pass?

Let's take a look at key elements of stakeholder engagement:

◊ Identify and prioritize key stakeholders in your ecosystem

◊ Ensure your communication strategies are aligned with your vision / core values

◊ Tailor communication strategies to effectively engage different stakeholder groups

◊ Align stakeholder interests with the overall vision and objectives of your business

Many modern authors have made significant contributions to the field of communication and leadership, influencing individuals and businesses alike. We have mentioned Simon Sinek several times already. He became well-known for his book *Start with Why*. Sinek emphasizes the importance of understanding the underlying purpose and motivation behind actions, which has resonated with countless leaders. Through his TED Talk and subsequent publications, Sinek inspired businesses like Apple and Southwest Airlines to articulate their "why," leading to stronger brand identities and increased customer loyalty.

Another influential figure is Brené Brown, renowned for her work on vulnerability, empathy, and shame resilience. Her books, including *Daring Greatly* and *Braving the Wilderness*, have provided invaluable insights for leaders seeking to foster inclusive and empathetic workplaces. Brown's research and teachings have been instrumental in transforming organizational cultures, as demonstrated by companies like Google and Microsoft, which have integrated her principles into their leadership development programs.

Extra Time: Brené Brown also has some pretty fantastic podcast episodes with members of the *Ted Lasso* cast... just sayin'.

In the realm of interpersonal communication, Susan Cain's book, *Quiet: The Power of Introverts in a World That Can't Stop Talking,* has had a profound impact. Cain's work highlights the strengths of introverted individuals and emphasizes the importance of creating environments that cater to different communication styles. Many businesses, such as Slack and Basecamp, have adopted practices that accommodate introverted team members, resulting in more inclusive and productive workspaces.

Daniel Pink's book, *To Sell Is Human,* explores the art of persuasion and influence in various aspects of life, including the workplace. Pink's research-backed insights on effective communication and motivation strategies have been applied by businesses like HubSpot and Salesforce to enhance sales and marketing efforts, leading to improved customer engagement and increased revenue.

These authors, among others, have provided valuable frameworks and strategies for effective communication in leadership. Through their works, they have influenced numerous individuals and businesses, enabling them to develop stronger, more inclusive, and purpose-driven cultures.

INFLUENCING SKILLS

"The key to successful leadership today is influence, not authority." —Ken Blanchard

Ted Lasso's influence as a coach extends far beyond the pitch. One of his key strengths lies in his ability to understand and adapt to different influencing styles and approaches. He recognizes that each player on the team responds differently to motivation and guidance. Whether it's offering words of encouragement, providing constructive feedback, or leading by example, Ted tailors his approach to resonate with each individual. This personalized touch not only fosters a sense of connection but also ensures that his message will be received and acted upon effectively.

Moreover, Ted places a strong emphasis on building trust and credibility within the team. He knows that trust is the cornerstone of any successful relationship, and he consistently demonstrates integrity, honesty, and reliability. Whether it's sticking to his word or standing up for his players, Ted's actions consistently align with his words, solidifying the trust his team places in him. This foundation of trust empowers him to influence decisions, strategies, and the overall team dynamic.

Each of us responds differently to motivation and guidance.

When it comes to using communication skills and conflict resolution, Ted employs a diplomatic and empathetic approach. He understands that conflicts are a natural part of any team dynamic, but he also believes that they present opportunities for growth and understanding. Ted encourages open communication and actively listens to the concerns of his players. Through calm and respectful discussions, he guides the team toward resolutions that benefit everyone. This inclusive approach not only strengthens team cohesion but also showcases Ted's mastery in influencing positive outcomes, both on and off the playing field.

In today's interconnected world, the power of influence is more pronounced than ever before. From locker rooms to board rooms, leaders who can effectively sway opinions and inspire action are invaluable. As we searched for ways to look at influencing skills, our inner Ted said this:

> *"Finding the answer is like searching for your glasses when they're perched right on your nose. Sometimes, you just need to cross your eyes and take a good look!"*

Right in front of us is today's influencer market, driven primarily by social media influencers. As of 2023, the size of the influencer market has grown to over $21 billion. That has more than doubled since 2020. The impact of social media influencers is undeniable. Take for example Kylie Jenner and her cosmetics brand, Kylie Cosmetics. Within a matter of months, Kylie Cosmetics reached sales figures in the tens of millions of dollars, largely driven by her social media influence.

As we search for parallels between Ted's leadership style and the world of social media influencers, it's fairly easy to uncover valuable lessons for leaders in any domain.

Be authentic and relatable

Ted Lasso's authenticity is his secret weapon. He approaches his role with genuine care for his players and staff. This genuineness builds trust and fosters a strong sense of camaraderie within the team. Similarly, successful social media influencers thrive on authenticity. They connect with their followers on a personal level, sharing their experiences, struggles, and triumphs. This relatability allows them to build a loyal and engaged audience.

Example: **Casey Neistat** is a prominent YouTuber, filmmaker, entrepreneur, and cultural influencer known for his distinctive style and significant impact on the digital media landscape. As of 2023, he has over 12.6 million subscribers on YouTube. Like Ted Lasso, his success is rooted in his ability to create a bond with his audience based on a genuine connection.

Casey Neistat's video "Do What You Can't" (with over 15 million views and counting) is a powerful and inspirational piece that encourages viewers to break free from societal norms and expectations, daring them to pursue their dreams and passions relentlessly. Through a dynamic and visually captivating narrative, Neistat exemplifies his own life journey as a testament to defying limitations and doubters, emphasizing the idea that achieving the seemingly impossible is within reach for those who refuse to be constrained by their fears or setbacks.

The video's impact lies in its ability to instill a sense of empowerment, motivating viewers to embrace challenges, overcome obstacles, and transform aspirations into reality, making it a source of motivation and inspiration for individuals striving to reach their full potential.

Show empathy and understanding

Ted Lasso is a master of understanding people's motivations and fears. He listens attentively and strives to meet individuals where they are. Influencers, too, possess the ability to empathize with their audience's needs and desires. By addressing these concerns, they become a trusted source of information and inspiration.

Example: **Kayla Itsines** is a well-known fitness trainer, author, and entrepreneur who has made a significant impact in the fitness and wellness industry. She gained widespread recognition and fame for her fitness programs and social media presence.

Kayla is known for opening up about her own personal experiences filled with struggles and challenges. In these experiences, she demonstrates empathy with her audience's struggles and creates a sense of relatability.

Provide positive reinforcement

(The Jamie Tartts of the world need this!)

Ted is a firm believer in the power of positivity. He uplifts his team, even in the face of adversity, reinforcing their self-belief. Likewise, social media influencers often serve as a source of positivity and encouragement. They motivate their followers to pursue their passions, overcome obstacles, and believe in themselves.

Example: **Nas Daily**, also known as Nuseir Yassin, has over 12 million subscribers on YouTube and is a popular content creator known for his one-minute videos that provide glimpses into the lives, cultures, and stories of people from around the world.

Known for global exploration, a central theme of his content is the celebration of humanity. He tells the stories of ordinary individuals with extraordinary experiences, shedding light on their challenges, accomplishments, and the universal aspects of the human condition.

Influence, whether on the football field or in the digital realm, hinges on genuine connection, empathy, and positive reinforcement. Not surprisingly, Ted Lasso's leadership style mimics real-world social media influencer superstars, and the lessons described above serve as a remarkable blueprint for anyone seeking to become an effective influencer, both in their professional and personal lives. By embracing authenticity and a deep understanding of others, leaders can build strong, engaged teams or communities that rally around a common vision.

So, as you navigate your own leadership journey, take a page from Ted's playbook, and remember that true influence comes from a place of genuine care and connection. That was his superpower in creating a team.

TEAMWORK

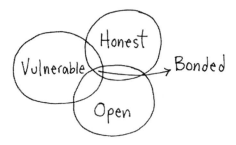

Previously on Ted Lasso...

Ted made it clear that team-building was one of his strategies for AFC Richmond. One by one he won over the hearts and minds of, well, everyone:

◊ The team: The new gaffers fixed the water pressure

◊ The staff: Yes, until we get a new Nate, you can assume you are our default Nate

◊ The leadership: Biscuits with the boss

◊ The press: Trent Crimm couldn't bring himself to root against Ted

◊ And eventually the entire town: Present during open practices

If you have ever sat through an awkward team-building activity or suggested that such a thing be considered "fluff," then Ted Lasso probably shed a light on the power of team-building done right. It seems obvious now – heck, it is even right inside the word... Team and Work must happen together to get *teamwork*.

So what are the elements of team-building that will allow for a team to work?

◊ Trust
◊ Effective communication
◊ Collaborative problem solving

◊ Conflict resolution and adaptability
◊ Allowing all voices to be heard
◊ Recognition and celebration
◊ Feedback
◊ Empowerment
◊ Shared values and purpose

That is a lot to ask of a movie night or a pillow fight! AFC Richmond's team-building activities went way beyond their official team nights. But none of them would have been possible if Ted hadn't first built trust.

Time out: Food for thought. Would that trust have ever come about if Nate had not outed Ted about his panic attacks? Ted took the opportunity to build trust by acknowledging his weaknesses and being vulnerable.

Obviously, TV accelerates natural timelines, but if Ted had read *The First 90 Days* by Michael D. Watkins, he definitely learned some of the critical lessons such as securing early wins (how about that shower water pressure) and stakeholder management. Through his honesty about not knowing European football, to his vulnerability and openness to learn from anyone, he built a foundation of trust. And once he had that trust, his team would do anything for him including learning the choreography to "Bye Bye Bye" by NSYNC as a parting gift to Dr. Fieldstone.

Ted knew that it would be a process to get the team to level up from movies nights to pillow fights, but he also knew that once they got there, there would be no turning back.

If you are looking to build teamwork, know that you do not have to be the leader of the entire team to inspire others. There are rope challenge courses, online scavenger hunts, virtual and live escape rooms, and trust walks that require collaboration and preparation. There are happy hours, potluck lunches or dinners, bowling nights, and Zoom coffee talks that can get folks engaged.

Ted knew to start small, and we would recommend the same. Here are a few team-building activities that we have participated in over the years:

◊ Two truths and a lie: Everyone submits two truths about themselves and a lie, and folks have to guess which is the lie. It is a fun way to learn about each other and hear all voices.

◊ Book banter: Everyone submits their favorite book and the team has to guess which book belongs to which person. Who knows, an informal book club might spring up from this!

◊ It could be as simple as bringing in your favorite homemade treat.

Again, successful team-building activities do not need to be hard. Done intentionally, they can be extremely powerful.

Team-building is proactive in its approach. It involves deliberately creating opportunities for team members to interact, collaborate, and develop stronger working relationships. Instead of waiting for conflicts or communication breakdowns to occur, proactive team-building aims to prevent these issues by fostering a positive and cohesive team dynamic from the outset.

Overall, proactive team building is about taking intentional steps to create a positive, collaborative, and high-functioning team. It's a strategic investment in the team's effectiveness and overall success.

EMPOWER A TEAM THROUGH COMMUNICATION

Ted Lasso and Roy Kent, though different in leadership styles, share a mutual respect and understanding for the game and their team.

Ted recognized Roy's potential as a leader early on and used specific strategies to empower him to take on a more prominent role.

First and foremost, Ted provided Roy with regular feedback—at times direct, other times creative (i.e., *A Wrinkle in Time* was a sneaky way to present the burden of leadership). Ted took the time to acknowledge Roy's strengths, both on and off the field, and also offered constructive criticism when necessary. This helped Roy understand areas where he excelled and where he could improve. Initially, Roy was hesitant about feedback, but over time, he began to appreciate the value of constructive criticism and embraced it as a means to grow as a player and leader.

Ted also empowered Roy by encouraging him to take ownership of his roles and responsibilities. He gave Roy the autonomy to make decisions on the field and trust his judgment. At first, Roy was apprehensive about this newfound responsibility. He had always been a team player, but now Ted was asking him to step up and take charge. With guidance and support, Roy gradually gained confidence in his leadership abilities, realizing that he had the experience and knowledge to make impactful decisions for the team.

Furthermore, Ted facilitated open and transparent communication channels, creating an environment where everyone felt comfortable expressing their thoughts and concerns. This was especially important for Roy, as he had a reputation for being direct and assertive. Ted encouraged Roy to channel his communication style in a way that would instead motivate and inspire his teammates. Roy learned how to effectively communicate his expectations and rally the team, using his directness to instill a sense of urgency and purpose.

Through these strategies, Ted not only recognized Roy's leadership potential but also provided him with the tools and opportunities to embrace it. Roy's transformation from a skilled player to a respected team leader was a testament to Ted's empowering leadership style and his ability to bring out the best in his players.

Together, they forged a partnership that not only elevated Roy's game but also contributed to the overall success and cohesion of AFC Richmond.

Business: NETFLIX

In the late 2000s, Netflix recognized the growing potential of streaming technology and made a strategic shift from a DVD rental-by-mail service to become a subscription-based streaming service. It's obvious that significant changes and investment with technology were needed and executed. However, the leadership team at Netflix also recognized that the company needed to fundamentally change how it operated and communicated to ultimately be successful.

In 2009, Netflix published its famous Culture Deck, a presentation document that outlined the company's core values and culture. This document, authored by Netflix CEO Reed Hastings and Chief Talent Officer Patty McCord, was made public and widely praised for its transparency. It emphasized values like "freedom and responsibility," where employees were empowered to make decisions and take ownership.

In the 2010s, Netflix continued its impressive growth by focusing on both content creation and global expansion. Creative freedom and risk-taking fostered innovation in storytelling, a culture that has been pivotal in attracting top talent in the entertainment industry. Similarly, the communication policy of openness and transparency played a significant role in navigating the challenges of content licensing and distribution on a global scale.

Interested in more readings on Communication and Influence?
Check out what might be on Beard's bookshelf...

- *Emotional Intelligence,* Daniel Goleman

- *Daring Greatly*, Brené Brown

- *Radical Candor*, Kim Scott

- *Quiet*, Susan Cain

- *To Sell Is Human,* Daniel Pink

7 ADAPTABILITY & RESILIENCE

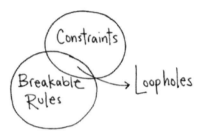

Previously on Ted Lasso...

In Season 1, Episode 10, Ted's son Henry asks him why it looks like he isn't doing anything during the game. Ted explains to Henry that in European football, he really isn't. He just has to "hope that all the coaching and training they've done during the week will let the team make the right decision when they're out on their own." He acknowledges that it's similar to being a parent. Parents, bosses, and coaches alike hope that all the training and coaching they have provided leads to adaptability and resilience on the pitch, in the board room, and in life.

Adaptability and resilience are essential to leadership. Leaders themselves need to be able to absorb data and information to pivot and make decisions. Their team needs to be able to do the same.

There are three key components to becoming a powerful force in this area:

◊   Embrace change and uncertainty
◊   Build resilience
◊   Problem solve and learn from feedback and failure

In 1970, NASA and the astronauts aboard Apollo 13 tested their skills of adaptability and resilience when an oxygen tank in the service module exploded approximately 56 hours into the mission. Having to abort, the entire focus shifted to safely returning the crew to Earth using a lunar module as a makeshift space lifeboat. The crew and ground control faced challenges, including maintaining life support, navigating their trajectory, and managing limited resources like power and water. Through extraordinary teamwork, innovative problem-solving, and unwavering determination, the crew and ground control managed to execute a series of critical maneuvers, ultimately bringing the Apollo 13 spacecraft safely back to Earth. The mission, while not achieving its original goal, stands as a remarkable testament to human ingenuity, adaptability, and resilience in the face of unimaginable adversity.

Embracing change and uncertainty was paramount in this dire situation. The mission's leaders, both in space and on Earth, demonstrated a growth mindset, viewing the evolving situation not as a threat, but as an opportunity for growth and problem-solving.

Throughout the crisis, building resilience in both the team and individuals was crucial. Leaders exemplified mental and emotional resilience in high-pressure situations, maintaining a positive outlook and demonstrating emotional intelligence.

They utilized structured problem-solving frameworks, even in situations with limited information, and weighed potential outcomes before taking action. Decisions were made with a clear understanding of the risks and the imperative to mitigate them.

Each character in *Ted Lasso* played a role in helping the AFC Richmond team and the individual players grow in terms of adaptability and resilience. Let's take a look at an example of how embracing change and overcoming the fear of uncertainty helped Keeley level up.

EMBRACING CHANGE AND UNCERTAINTY

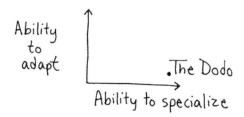

Ability to adapt

.The Dodo

Ability to specialize

"Change is the only constant in life." —Heraclitus

Keeley's leadership style is characterized by her supportive and collaborative approach. Heraclitus's quote aligns with Keeley's belief in the importance of being adaptable and open to new experiences and challenges. She recognizes that in order to thrive and succeed, individuals and teams must be willing to navigate and embrace change. Embracing change allows for growth, improvement, and the opportunity to adapt to new circumstances.

Keeley learned many lessons along the way, including a powerful one from Rebecca to be a lion not a panda. It was not the only lesson that Rebecca would teach as she became a mentor when Keeley opened her own PR firm. Many of those lessons involved how to grab an opportunity and maximize it. Rebecca believed you shouldn't let fear of the unknown (or anything else, for that matter) stop you from accomplishing your dreams.

If you have been anywhere near the internet this year, then you certainly have heard of technological advancements around artificial intelligence (AI). It is no question that there are positive and negative possibilities surrounding the use of AI. Those who choose to ignore (or let fear interfere with) this reality will find themselves left behind. We can imagine Ted saying: *"That would be like my grandfather refusing to learn how his new TV remote control works."*

Being willing to step into the unknown allows for learning and growth. We all need to lean in to the unfamiliar to become better versions of ourselves.

RESILIENCE FOR YOU AND YOUR TEAM

A good deal about becoming better versions of ourselves revolves around overcoming our own fears – of change, of belief (Impostor Syndrome rearing its ugly head again), and of failure...

It is interesting to think about the personal and business implications of building resilience. Dr. Sharon Fieldstone was unquestionably one of the unsung heroes for AFC Richmond. As the team's sports psychologist, she helped players and coaches develop strategies to work through their issues. This helped to develop individual coping mechanisms and strategies to weather high-pressure situations.

Businesses need to build the same type of resilience. In the way that therapists help individuals by listening and questioning, businesses need to listen to their stakeholders and question the right next steps... especially when life throws lemons.

One of our favorite quotes from Ted Lasso is "never bring an umbrella to a brainstorm." We have talked about the importance of having a vision and purpose and a culture to support that. Open

"Never bring an umbrella to a brainstorm."

communication is the conduit by which organizations learn, grow, and succeed. So if an organization is to become resilient, it must not be so set in its ways that it gets stuck or panics (because paralysis can cause the Y-ps!).

"If you always do what you always did,
you will always get what you always got."
—Henry Ford

Brainstorming is a critical element in working through hard times.

Think about Dr. Sharon's role. She created a safe place for team members to have an open dialogue about their problems. There was no judgment, and all emotions and ideas were validated. While we were never witness to a session with the good doctor, we believe that there was a lot of brainstorming and problem-solving ideas to help the players learn to adapt. That is the role that brainstorming and open lines of communication can play in any organization.

Resilience is often an outcome in dealing with adversity.

In Season 2, Episode 8, titled "Man City," Coach Lasso faces a difficult situation when he has to deliver a halftime pep talk to motivate his team during a crucial match against powerhouse Manchester City. Richmond is trailing, and the odds seem insurmountable.

During this halftime speech, Ted doesn't resort to the usual motivational clichés. Instead, he decides to tell a heartfelt and personal story. He opens up about a difficult time in his own life when he faced a daunting challenge and was struggling to find his way. He talked about his divorce and the pain he felt.

Rather than relying on clichés, Ted uses his experiences to inspire and unite.

Ted's vulnerability and honesty in this moment surprises and touches his players and coaching staff. He used his own life experience to convey the message that even in the face of adversity, it's possible to come back stronger. He tells his team that life is full of "twists and turns, bobbles and weaves," and it's essential to keep moving forward, supporting each other.

This powerful speech helps the team to regain their confidence and motivation. They go back onto the field with renewed energy and manage to secure an unexpected draw (tie) against Manchester City, a team that was expected to dominate them.

Ted doesn't rely on typical sports clichés but instead connects with his players on a deeper level, using his own experiences to inspire and unite them. Showing vulnerability has that power.

Let's see what that looks like and why.

PROBLEM-SOLVING & DECISION-MAKING
IN UNCERTAIN TIMES

In the realm of leadership, there's an irrefutable truth: Uncertainty is the only constant. Whether you're facing a market downturn, a sudden technological shift, or a global crisis, the ability to navigate through uncertain times with precision is a hallmark of exceptional leadership. In this section, we'll delve into the crucial skills of problem-solving and decision-making, and how employing structured frameworks can be your compass in the storm.

When we first started our company, Lifecycle Insights, our marketing plan was to attend conferences and industry events to meet as many people as possible. We knew that by listening to the needs of our prospects and customers, we would be able to not just share with them how our product could help them but also hear their needs so we could build a better product.

We launched on Halloween 2019. Five months later, our worlds went into lockdown due to the pandemic. We, like every other business, had to find ways to be resilient and develop new strategies for achieving our business plan.

There are many brainstorming techniques to help individuals and businesses think flexibly about a situation or adversity in order to find potential solutions and develop resilience. One that would have made for the best business meeting ever would be the journalist questioning activity delivered by Trent Crimm of *The Independent* (or Keeley Jones, The Independent Woman!).

In this activity the team looks at their current situation and asks themselves the "5 Ws and 1 H" that a reporter would ask. They then consider the change or challenges they are presently facing, and answer the questions now viewed with a new lens.

Here's what it might look like to consider our sales and marketing strategy Trent Crimm style:

Question	Current (pre-lockdown)	Future (after lockdown)
Who?	Sales/marketing team	Sales/marketing team
What?	Live conferences and events	Webinars, podcasts, and social media
When?	Quarterly (they are expensive!)	At least twice a month (they are free!)
Where?	Around the country	Online
Why?	Meeting people face to face gives the team the opportunity to hear the needs of prospects and educate them on our solution. Thousands of prospects and clients go to events to learn.	Being unable to meet folks live at events means that people will need to learn strategies for improving their businesses in a different way. Providing educational content in bite-sized, online formats can help their learning and help provide us feedback on their needs and how we can help.
How?	Clever booths with swag to attract attention and start conversations. Try to maximize the number of people we engage with.	Partner with other companies who work with the same prospects to help educate them on how to grow their businesses. Integrate this conversation with how our solution can help. Create online communities where our customers can provide feedback. Build the product based on the feedback to ensure raving fans who will share our solution with folks in their peer groups.

Part of the power of brainstorming is that you develop the skill and muscle to try alternate approaches in problem solving.

If Ted Lasso did a talk on adaptability and resilience, he would no doubt mention one of his Lassoisms: "Taking on a challenge is a lot like riding a horse, isn't it? If you're comfortable while you're doing it, you're probably doing it wrong."

Demonstrating those skills is easy when you see examples of them. But as Ted's alter-ego Led Tasso showed us, sometimes it is the counter-example that really drives home the point.

Business: BLOCKBUSTER

While platforms like Netflix transitioned to online streaming, Blockbuster continued to focus on physical stores for its video rentals. This reluctance to adapt to emerging technologies and changing consumer preferences was a critical misstep.

When Netflix introduced its DVD-by-mail service and later shifted to streaming, Blockbuster initially viewed them as minor competitors. This delay in acknowledging the threat allowed Netflix to gain a significant market foothold. By the time Blockbuster attempted to enter the online rental space, it was already playing catch-up, and its efforts were too little, too late.

Blockbuster's aggressive expansion strategy, which involved opening numerous stores worldwide, left the company burdened with substantial debt. When the brick-and-mortar rental industry began to decline due to digital advancements, Blockbuster found itself financially strained and unable to sustain its extensive network of stores. This over-extension further weakened the company's ability to adapt to the changing landscape.

This case serves as a stark example of the importance of adaptability and resilience in the face of evolving markets and technologies.

At the end of Season 1, AFC Richmond faced relegation if they lost to Manchester City. It looked bleak. Everyone Ted ran into told him, "It's the hope that kills you."

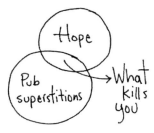

Ted looked everywhere for ideas on how they could beat Man City. He went so far as to tell Rebecca that when it doesn't go well, she could fire him. He thought they might need a "proper" football coach. In turn, she told him that every disadvantage has its advantage. Since Ted was not a "proper" football coach, he was able to see things differently, which can create confusion. This gave Ted the brilliant idea to create chaos with a litany of trick plays.

Ted gathers the team around the whiteboard and has them brainstorm any trick plays (ahem, elaborate set pieces) they have ever tried on a pitch. The team is inspired to think outside the box. In the face of reality that traditional formations wouldn't work, AFC Richmond surprised the world. They adapted and created a little chaos of their own.

One of the most powerful elements of that episode was that the entire team contributed ideas. If it "takes a village to raise a child," it "takes ideas from players of a dozen nations to tie Man City."

Thinking outside the box, the pitch, and the playbook are great ways to begin problem solving.

Interested in more readings on Adaptability and Resilience? Check out what might be on Beard's bookshelf...

- *Hundred Percenters,* Mark Murphy

- *Reality is Broken,* Jane McGonigal

- *Atomic Habits,* James Clear

- *Leading Change,* John P. Kotter

- *The Road Less Stupid,* Keith J. Cunningham

8 NETWORK & COMMUNITY

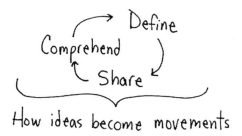

How ideas become movements

Whether you are just embarking on your leadership journey or are already a seasoned leader in some realm... building and leveraging a network is key to ensuring the success of your vision.

As the saying goes: "Your network is your net worth." The leadership elements demonstrated in *Ted Lasso* and outlined in the preceding chapters are simply not possible without the support of a network.

Malcolm Gladwell, author of *Tipping Point*, would describe a person's network as a complex web of social connections and relationships that shape their access to information, resources, and opportunities. One of the key points in his book is that networks play a crucial role in influencing an individual's success and outcomes in various aspects of life, including professional endeavors.

Just as in leadership, in the same way your core values are at the center of what you do, you are at the core of your network. You are surrounded by your immediate support group – family, friends, and your Diamond Dogs!

At the next level in your network are the folks with whom you work, live, and play day-to-day. Beyond that is your broader network which has varying reach.

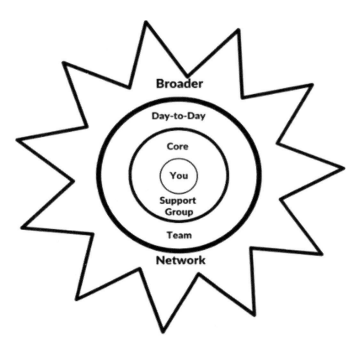

This is easy to conceptualize for yourself (or even for Ted!). It gets more complicated when you realize that every person on the planet is at the core of their own network.

This is critical for effective leadership because networks facilitate the flow of information, resources, and support. They enable leaders to influence and persuade others, to adapt to changing circumstances, and to make a meaningful impact on organizations and communities. Cultivating and nurturing networks is a strategic imperative for leaders in today's interconnected world.

The importance of networks in leadership can be understood through several key aspects. In a not-so shocking turn of events, we will demonstrate these aspects by examining the networks of *Ted Lasso* characters.

Area	Description	*Ted Lasso characters*
Information Flow and Access	Networks provide leaders with access to a vast amount of information and resources. Leaders can tap into their network to gather insights, data, and perspectives that can inform their decision-making processes. This access to information can be invaluable in making well-informed and strategic decisions.	Rebecca's network is wide. She was able to use her resources to acquire a tabloid-like photo of Ted and Keeley, and with a single call, she was also able to ensure that photo never went to press.
Influence and Persuasion	Leadership often involves persuading and influencing others to support a particular vision or goal. Having a strong network can enhance a leader's ability to build relationships, gain allies, and convince others to follow their lead. This is especially important in situations where formal authority may be limited.	Edwin Okufu, the Nigerian billionaire who wanted Sam to join his team, used his extensive network to make sure Sam did not make the Nigerian national team (and had a really rough night at his restaurant).
Resource Mobilization	Leaders need resources to achieve their objectives, whether it's financial capital, human resources, or technical expertise. Networks can facilitate the mobilization of these resources by connecting leaders with individuals or organizations willing to contribute to the cause.	Rupert used his networking powers for good at the charity auction and drove in record donations. Then he used those same powers for bad by attempting to embarrass Rebecca by canceling her band.

Problem Solving / Innovation	Networks bring together people with diverse backgrounds, skills, and experiences. This diversity can be a source of creative problem-solving and innovation. Leaders who cultivate diverse networks are more likely to find unique solutions to complex challenges.	One of our favorite scenes of all time was when Ted and Coach Beard asked their very international team to list all of the trick plays they had ever learned.
Personal Development	Leadership is a continuous journey of personal growth and development. Networks can provide mentors, coaches, and advisors who can offer guidance, feedback, and support to leaders as they navigate their roles and responsibilities.	Ted used Roy as part of his network to help Isaac become the captain he knew he could be. (And maybe just maybe, Ted was using Isaac to show Roy the coach he could become. ☺)
Building Trust and Credibility	A leader's network can vouch for their credibility and trustworthiness. When others see that a leader is connected to respected individuals or organizations, it can enhance their own reputation and legitimacy.	Would Nate have ever been able to shop for a posh suit if Keeley hadn't vouched for him?
Adaptation and Resilience	In a rapidly changing world, leaders must be adaptive and resilient. Networks serve as a safety net of support during challenging times. Leaders with strong networks may have access to alternative options and solutions when faced with adversity.	Throughout the show, Dr. Sharon became an important part of Ted's network – helping him develop a resilience he didn't know he had.

Global Perspective	In a globalized world, leadership often involves dealing with international issues and stakeholders. Networks that extend beyond national borders can provide leaders with a global perspective, helping them navigate complex international relationships and challenges.	Sam used his star power on the pitch to draw attention to political atrocities.
Community and Social Impact	Leadership is not just about personal success; it's also about making a positive impact on society. Networks can connect leaders with like-minded individuals and organizations working toward similar social or environmental goals, amplifying their collective impact.	The entire show of *Ted Lasso* has helped to shed light on the importance of mental health.
Legacy / Succession Planning	Leaders often think about their legacy and the continuity of their work. A well-established network can be instrumental in identifying and grooming potential successors or ensuring the sustainability of an organization or initiative.	Rebecca's character arc really grew since the first season. She went from trying to destroy the team to selling 49% of the club to the fans – a fabulous legacy to create and enjoy.

Let's not forget Rule #1 – Leadership Is Life! Your network is what breathes oxygen into your ability to lead.

THERE ARE NO NPCS
(NON-PLAYER CHARACTERS)

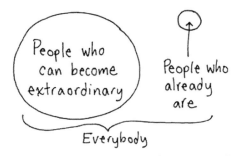

The reach of a network dramatically varies based on the behaviors of the person at the core. This leads to two important ideas:

1. There are no NPCs in this world.

2. How you treat anyone is how you treat everyone.

NPC is an acronym originating from the world of gaming, referring to characters that are controlled by the game's artificial intelligence rather than by a human player. They serve various roles within the gaming environment, from providing information to offering challenges or interactions for the player-controlled character.

In the broader context of leadership and teamwork, the term has been humorously borrowed to emphasize the importance of recognizing every individual's unique contributions and potential for innovation within an organization.

Everyone is a lead character in their own life!

This theme challenges the notion that some individuals are merely background characters, asserting that everyone has the potential to shape their own destiny (and become the best versions of themselves). Everyone is the lead character in their own life!

Free Guy is a movie that catapults us into the bustling metropolis of Free City, a virtual realm teeming with players and non-player characters (NPCs). At the heart of this tale is Guy (played by Ryan

Reynolds), an NPC who, through a series of extraordinary events, discovers his own agency. He transforms from a passive background character to an active participant in his own story.

This transformation is a testament to the idea that no one is bound by a predetermined role. Just as Guy defied expectations and asserted his autonomy, so too can individuals in real life seize the reins of their own narratives. The film serves as a powerful reminder that each person possesses the potential to be a protagonist – not just a supporting player – in their own life story.

Through Ted's unwavering positivity, genuine care for his players, and a keen understanding of those players' unique strengths, Ted empowers each member of his team to rise above perceived limitations. This mirrors the theme of "no NPCs" in the sense that every player, regardless of initial role or background, has the potential to become a driving force in the team's success.

Both *Free Guy* and *Ted Lasso* underscore the profound impact that belief, encouragement, and opportunity can have on an individual's journey. They challenge the notion that some people are destined to be secondary characters, asserting that everyone has the power to shape their own narrative.

Whether it's Guy discovering his inner hero in a virtual world or Ted Lasso coaching his team to success on the playing field, these narratives serve as poignant reminders that there are no NPCs in life. Each of us, with the right support and mindset, is the protagonist of our own story.

> *How people treat those they perceive as "lesser" can be a strong indicator of their true nature.*

It is important for each individual to also reflect on what this means in how we treat others. Richard Branson, maverick entrepreneur and founder of Virgin Group, has a unique approach to assessing how individuals treat others. One of his methods involves enlisting his father to play the role of a chauffeur for potential business partners. By doing so, Branson gains a firsthand perspective on how these individuals interact with those they might consider "beneath" them in a hierarchical context (treating them like NPCs!). This unconventional test is a powerful way to uncover true character traits that might not be readily apparent in a traditional business setting.

Branson recognizes that how individuals treat those they perceive as "lesser" can be a strong indicator of their true nature. By incorporating this unconventional test into his assessment of potential partners, he underscores the significance of empathy and respect in building meaningful relationships, a philosophy that has undoubtedly contributed to his own remarkable success as a leader and entrepreneur. (Ted Lasso would ace that test!) Through this unique approach, Richard Branson emphasizes the importance of genuine human connections in business.

CONNECTORS & PEER GROUPS

Keeley Jones, our favorite public relations expert, shines a different light on the value of connecting with one's network. Keeley's leadership revolves around building and nurturing relationships, both within the team and with external stakeholders. She actively seeks out mentors and advisors, recognizing the wealth of insights and opportunities they offer. Keeley's involvement in events and the community showcases the power of leveraging one's professional network for growth and success. Her approach embodies the essence of connecting with your network to fuel personal and organizational development.

Author Malcolm Gladwell would categorize Keeley as a "Connector." In his book *The Tipping Point,* Gladwell shares that Connectors are individuals who possess an extraordinary ability to forge connections and build relationships with a wide and diverse range of people. They have an extensive network that spans various social circles, allowing them to link individuals who might not otherwise come into contact. Connectors are the social hubs in a community, serving as bridges between different groups, and facilitating the flow of information.

One of the defining characteristics of a Connector is their innate talent for cultivating and maintaining relationships. They are naturally outgoing, friendly, and approachable, which makes it easy for them to establish connections with others. Connectors thrive on social interactions and are genuinely interested in getting to know people from all walks of life. They possess a genuine curiosity about others and are skilled listeners, which enables them to learn about people's interests, needs, and aspirations.

> *Connectors possess a genuine curiosity about others and are skilled listeners.*

Connectors play a crucial role in the spread of information and ideas within a community or society. They act as conduits for knowledge, sharing insights, recommendations, and opportunities with their extensive network. Because of their widespread connections, Connectors have the power to accelerate the spread of trends, innovations, and social movements.

Keeley's success stems from hard work in using her network to make connections for her clients. That is how she is able to hand out free espresso coffeemakers to each of the players as a perk for their marketing efforts. And she is savvy enough to use their star power to expand the user base of the newest dating app, Bantr.

Have you heard the saying, "It's not what you know but who you know?" Connectors prove that to be true.

But it is not just about knowing lots of people. It is about knowing what makes them tick... like Ted asking Keeley about Jamie's operating instructions. And here is the big secret that Connectors and every single sales and marketing coach will tell you. In connecting with people, provide them value. Yep! As author Joe Polish titled his book, focus on *What's in It for Them?*

> *It's not just who you know... it's knowing what makes them tick.*

This is very much the approach we took in growing our company Lifecycle Insights. When the world went remote and we could not plan on live events, we reset our thinking. We knew we had a small audience and would need the help of other larger companies to co-market with us in order to grow our audience.

Through some connections, we came up with creative marketing ideas, like streaming an educational webinar on YouTube called Jurassic SOC, a parody of Jurassic Park in the realm of cybersecurity that entertained and educated our market. We offered to do as much of the heavy lifting for the event as we could – writing scripts, creating marketing campaigns, organizing the meetings and action items. In exchange, the larger companies brought the crowd. By leveraging large companies (our network), we increased our webinar audience from an average of 100 to over 2,000 people.

Once we were able to travel to live events again, we continued to grow through the power of networking and the idea of providing value to others. At one of our favorite industry events, we were given a copy of the book *Go Giver* by Bob Burg and John David Mann. This book is a parable about the "Five Laws of Stratospheric Success." These laws emphasize the importance of giving without expectation, adding value to others' lives, and building genuine, lasting relationships.

That particular event was a peer group for IT business owners. The philosophy surrounding the event aligned to the principles of Go Giving. We have seen this work for ourselves and for the CEOs and business owners who participate in peer groups. Peer groups can become a part of your Diamond Dogs or an extra layer of support.

Some of the benefits received from peer groups:

◊ Provide diverse perspectives and insights from individuals with varying experiences and backgrounds

◊ Share knowledge, skills, and best practices within a supportive and collaborative environment

◊ Promote accountability and motivation, encouraging members to set and achieve goals

◊ Facilitate networking and the exchange of valuable contacts and connections

◊ Offer a sense of belonging and camaraderie, reducing feelings of isolation and fostering a community of like-minded individuals

◊ Create opportunities for personal and professional growth through shared learning and development experiences

◊ Act as a source of constructive feedback, helping members identify blind spots and areas for improvement

Peer groups are not only effective for business owners. They can have a positive impact at any stage in someone's career. Finding true peers to serve as a source of inspiration and motivation is another way to help individuals level up to a better version of themselves.

Students, recent graduates, or folks who are interested in a career change can greatly benefit from the power of peer groups. The connections broaden their network and can help them brainstorm next steps along their journey. New employees in a large company can often feel overwhelmed or get lost in the layers and politics of an organization. Peer groups help to overcome that.

Penalty Kick: Peer groups are not the same as peer pressure! If Keeley had let her friendship with Shandy continue to negatively influence the direction of her PR firm, things might have turned out very differently. That is one of the reasons that it is also important to have mentors in your life. Keeley certainly did.

MENTORS

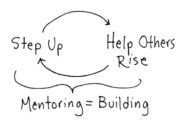

Step Up   Help Others Rise

Mentoring = Building

One of the most powerful (and delightful, if you ask us) relationships in the show is the one between Keeley and Rebecca. Since we loved the scene when Keeley "interviewed" Roy Kent as several iterations of Keeley Jones, The Independent Woman, we imagined what it would be like to interview Keeley about her connection with Rebecca.

Reporter: Keeley, you and Rebecca have a unique connection. How would you describe it?

Keeley: Ooh, she's magical... and *tall!* I once asked if I should be a lion or a panda. She's a lion – a real force of nature – but a compassionate one. She's my best friend and mentor all rolled into one!

Reporter: How did the mentorship begin?

Keeley: At first she terrified me, but I think she saw some potential in me. She always has great advice... and well, I think she needed a friend. She's done so many things. There's a lot I can learn from her.

Reporter: What is the most valuable lesson you learned from Rebecca?

Keeley: To believe in myself. Confidence. That, and being accountable is important.

Reporter: What has Rebecca's mentorship inspired you to do?

Keeley: Well, it inspired me to start my PR firm. Oooooh, and I wrote a proposal for a women's football team in Richmond!

Reporter: Is there anything else you would like to share about mentoring?

Keeley: Well, one thing that actually Higgins taught me... I was so scared to tell Rebecca that I was leaving the club to start my PR firm. He said the best thing. "Good mentors know you might leave. Great mentors hope you do!"

There are certainly lots of examples of mentoring and (obviously) coaching and advising relationships throughout the series. Roy and Jamie were a most entertaining pair from head butts to 4:00 AM training to bicycling lessons in Amsterdam.

In all of the relationships, we got to see several of the powerful qualities of mentoring:

◊   **Guidance and support**: Mentors share their experiences and expertise in the form of advice and feedback.

◊   **Personal growth and development**: Mentors encourage goal setting and skill development.

◊   **Inspiration and accountability**: Mentors help mentees see what their full potential could be and have direct and honest conversations to keep them working toward that.

We talked about the power of Go Giving, and mentoring is certainly one example of that. However, there are benefits for the mentor as well. Witnessing the growth of their mentees is highly rewarding and can provide a great sense of purpose. It helps mentors improve and refine their leadership and communication skills. They broaden their own network and perspectives. It is also an opportunity to really build their legacy.

There are official mentoring programs, although many times mentoring relationships grow from connections individuals make along the way. It is one of the many potential outcomes of connecting and networking, as we will see in the next section.

NETWORKING

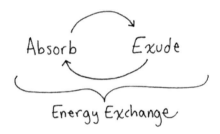

Prior to the rise of social media platforms, building your network was not for the faint of heart – especially for those of us who find social interaction with relative strangers difficult. It used to be that the most efficient way to build out your network was to participate in in-person events. Examples of such networking events include attending conferences, joining professional associations and clubs and groups, volunteering, and actively participating in alumni associations.

These in-person events were, and still are, a great way to meet up with like-minded people who can help you expand and call on your network in times of need. They offer face-to-face interactions and opportunities for more personal connections. In-person events allow people to build trust and rapport more easily, make memorable impressions, and observe body language and nonverbal cues – which can be critical to establishing a connection. In-person networking programs, like peer groups or chamber leads groups, seek to connect you with peers and advisors.

In the digital realm, there are certainly networking sites that support professional and personal networking. Their aim is to connect you with the components you would need to level up. In some of the strictly social networking sites, their goal is to just make the human-to-human connection. In the more professional focused or job board type sites, they aim to connect you with opportunities or others who have similar interests.

Each of those groups has a purpose, but the power of networking is multiplied when all of those elements are tied together. Your professional network might only know you as an "engineer" instead of a world-class problem solver aiming to work on creative projects at a startup. Your social site might only know that you run your daughter's Girl Scout troop, and not realize that you are looking for a mentor to help you grow your marketing coaching business. And none of them might really highlight the power of your military experience or the skills you bring to any organization.

A great network really does tie everything together. Let's take a look at the potential power of a great network:

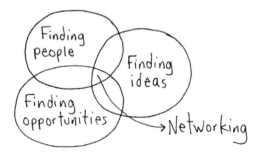

"Networking is not about just connecting people.
It's about connecting people with people,
people with ideas, and people with opportunities."
—Michele Jennae

Reflecting on the success of our company, we understand the positive impact networking had in making that happen.

◊ **Contacts/peers:** Of the four founders of our company, three had worked together and two had played volleyball together for years. Keeping relationships and contacts clearly made a difference. We grew our network of co-marketing collaborators through contacts we met along the way. Peer groups were valuable resources in making additional connections and providing feedback.

◊ **Mentors/coaches**: As we grew the business, we relied on mentors from our previous experiences. We used our own experiences to coach our team members. One of our former bosses coached us in business finance and helped to ensure a successful acquisition.

◊ **Interest groups/communities**: We found our prospects through interest groups on social media and at industry events. We were even honored by being given the Go Giver award at one of these events.

◊ **Information/resources**: With a small team, we had to use our resources wisely. In a vendor community, we would often trade reviewing or creating content for a fellow vendor for graphic design work.

◊ **Opportunities**: By creating relationships, our opportunities multiplied in ways we would not have expected. Marnie ended up co-authoring two other books with experts in the IT/Managed Services industry. We regularly have the opportunity to speak at events around the power of customer success and how you can use Go Giving to grow your business. We have stopped tracking the number of webinars, podcasts, and live streams that have hosted us. On the other end of the networking spectrum, the majority of the people we have hired came as a referral from our network. From our employees' perspective, that means their network got them an opportunity as well.

If you are a leader in a company, then there is a good chance that much of this rings familiar. If you are just entering the workforce (or parenting someone about to launch), then the idea of building your network might sound overwhelming. Would Ted say, *"It isn't as overwhelming as flying from Kansas to London to coach a game you have never played before"*? Who knows. But we do know that with the power of Ted's network, he was quite successful.

In The Game section, we will walk through some tactical strategies you can use to create, enhance, or grow your network. But first, let's work on leveling up!

Interested in more readings on Networking and Community? Check out what might be on Beard's bookshelf...

- *The Power of Five,* John Maxwell

- *Connected,* James H. Fowler and Nicholas Christakis

- *Radical Candor,* Kim Scott

- *The Go Giver,* Bob Burg and John David Mann

- *Multipliers,* Liz Wiseman

9 LEGACY & LEVELING UP

In this final section of training (you should be good and warmed up by now), we will dig into the ideas of legacy and leveling up.

> *"Be kind to everyone on the way up.*
> *You'll meet the same people on the way down."*
> *—Wilson Miznor, Hollywood playwright*

That quote certainly could have resonated with Roy as he battled with Jamie Tartt in Season 1. Ted talked to Roy about his feelings toward Jamie. Roy described him as a "bitchy prima donna." Ted asked Roy what he had been like when he was a young football star. Roy agreed, he had also been a "bitchy prima donna." That was a lightbulb moment for Roy. He realized that when he was just starting in the league, he also hated the "old guy" on the team who had once been considered legendary. Roy was watching his own progression flash right in front of him.

Now Roy's transformation (or character arc) didn't happen immediately. It took several more rounds with Jamie, lots of chats with Keeley, and some harsh words from Nate to get him there, but eventually Roy realized that he had peaked as a football player. Like many athletes, as they pass their prime years, Roy struggled with what that meant for him. Eventually, Ted "had him at Coach." Roy saw a new way he could level up and still give back to the game of football and its community that he loved.

If you want to relive some of how *Ted Lasso* made you feel, rewatch Roy's press conference in Season 3, Episode 9, when he explains why what Isaac did to the fan was wrong but he still gives him love.

(We're not crying, you're crying.) Roy indeed grew beyond his days on the pitch as a player and is now inspiring us as a coach.

Earlier, we talked about how the path to leveling up very much depended on two things...

Even more important to think about is that once you get where you want to be, you then need to realize that you aren't finished. It is just time to set a new goal and level up again.

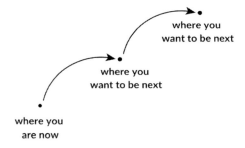

In the *Infinite Game*, Simon Sinek discussed a guide for leadership with an infinite mindset – of having pursuit of such a just vision that we dive toward the work to create greater meaning in our life. (Rule #1, baby! *Leadership Is Life!*)

As we lace up our boots (or cleats or sneakers or strappy sandals), and march onward and forward, we add footprints along the way. (Now for the love of Nate, do not leave those footprints on his grass!) It is not just about the goals we score, but about the way we influence this game of life for those who follow. Our legacies will not just be about the wins and losses. It will be about how we left the game for others.

LEVELING UP AND GROWTH

In the land of games, when it comes to winning, losing, and leveling up, we naturally think of video games. Jane McConigal, gamer, game designer, and author of *Reality Is Broken*, talks a lot about the power of leveling up and the power of gamification in our everyday lives.

Video games in particular are compelling to people because they provide:

◊ Social connection
◊ Positive emotions around accomplishment
◊ Challenging (yet achievable) tasks
◊ Clear goals and feedback
◊ Epic meaning (something larger than themselves)
◊ Make failures fun

The only way to level up in a game is to acquire new resources, skills, or teammates. This sounds a lot like what you would need to do to get a promotion. (Or to keep AFC Richmond from relegation!)

It is possible to imagine that life would be a lot easier, or at least more entertaining, if we were all characters on *Ted Lasso* (and no, you may not call dibs on being Roy Kent). Or maybe as a leading character in a light-hearted rom-com where everything works out in the end. However, that isn't the way life goes.

In reality, we prefer it this way because if life just happened to us, we would be like non-player characters (NPCs) in video games. We would just be going through the motions. The vision wouldn't be our own. We would merely be a cog in someone else's operating system.

Lucky for us, we get to write our own set of instructions and chart the path toward our vision.

Creating that path is exactly the next step a leader needs to take in order to see the vision come to fruition.

Let's think about Ted's vision to build a team. He knew Roy would be the first domino who needed to fall. From there, Roy could help unite the locker room. Once the team trusted each other, he laid out the four key elements for success. Well, he actually held the fourth one back a bit, but he believed in it all along...

◊   Conditioning
◊   Versatility
◊   Awareness
◊   Believe

Think about the strategies Ted, Coach Beard, and Roy (and eventually Nate again) implemented. They coached wind sprints for the team to work on conditioning. They drew names of other players and switched positions with them to learn the game from a fresh perspective. Roy even suggested a questionable string activity that made them each excruciatingly aware of where they were in relation to their teammates. And all along, believing in Believe was a theme.

> *"Vision without action is merely a dream.*
> *Action without vision just passes the time.*
> *Vision with action can change the world."*
> —*Joel Arthur Barker*

We had a vision to grow our company Lifecycle Insights through Raving Fans:

◊   Build the best damn reporting mechanism for MSPs
◊   Be everywhere in the space

◊   Ensure our customers' success by helping their customers be successful

Our leadership team then took the vision and added actions, metrics, and strategies to build the roadmap to success:

Vision	Strategies
Build the best damn reporting mechanism for MSPs	Get weekly feedback from our customers and keep building what they need
Be everywhere in the space	Social media, webinars, events
Ensure our customers' success by helping their customers be successful	Focus on providing insights their customers need – teach them how to deliver business outcomes for their clients

Earlier we took a look at how critical it is for a leader to have vision and purpose. More importantly, we talked about how you need to be very specific and clear about what that vision looks like. Check out these pairs of vision statements. We bet you will agree that they are the same, but different (SMARTer, you could say):

Vision 1: Lose weight this year.
Vision 2: By October 15th, I will lose 18 pounds and 2 inches around my waist.

Vision 1: Our company will grow and scale this year.
Vision 2: By December 30, 2025, our company will be generating $1M in annual recurring revenue.

Vision 1: I will get a job and save some money.
Vision 2: I will get a job in my field that allows me to save $10k and pay off my college debt within five years.

Once you have clarity on that SMART vision statement, the next step is to set long-term and short-term goals that create the path to success.

When (not if) your vision is reality in three years, what would that look like (be specific!)?

To hit that goal, ask yourself:

"What do I need to accomplish by a year from now?"

Then ask:

"What are three goals I could tackle in the next quarter?"

And finally:

"What does that mean I need to do this week?"

It would be nice if the process was more complicated than that, wouldn't it? That would give all of us a good excuse for why we aren't reaching our goals. *Reality check: Don't forget our Rules!* Onward. Forward... Stop getting in your own way... Defeat the blank page... Plan your work, then work your plan...

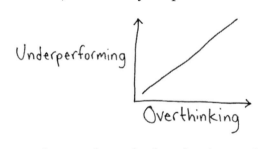

Ted was pretty passionate about the fact that it wasn't the hope that kills you. It was the *lack of hope*. Innovative filmmaker James Cameron would add, "Hope is not a strategy."

The first time kit man Nate had an idea for a strategic play, he mumbled, lacking enough confidence to say the words. Ted told him, "I have a hard time hearing people who don't believe in themselves." So when you write your goals, have confidence that they will put you on the path to your vision and then, by golly, make it happen.

Writing everything down, clarifying your goals and actions, and having a strategy in place all help to establish your path to success. However, for growth to actually happen, you need to take those steps and follow that path. Things don't always happen as smoothly as a sit-com plot. Sometimes…

◊ A "Sam" gets walked over and needs to work on standing his or her ground.

◊ A "Rupert" shows up and tries to lead with fear.

◊ A "Nate" loses his or her way and has to go back to the very beginning.

As you think about leveling up, consider the areas where you need growth. From technical skills to mental health work, you need to create a path for growth that will help you become the best version of yourself.

Now that we have looked at defining the path, it's important to track your progress along the way.

KEEPING SCORE

What is inspected is what is expected.

Whistle! Whistle! Read that again. What is inspected is what is expected.

It reminds us of the famous quote credited to Albert Einstein: "The definition of insanity is doing the same thing over and over again and expecting different results." If you are not keeping score on where you stand and how it relates to where you are heading, how will you know you are going to get there?

I expect...	I should inspect...
To lose 40 pounds	My weight weekly to track progress
To level up on a video game (or Duolingo!)	My points and progress (and badges!)
To get into a good college	My SAT or ACT score, my grades, my community service
To get a promotion	My resume, experiences, certifications, and skills
To get a job	Opportunities and their alignment to my core values
To have a mentor	Authorities in my network

Once you know what you are aiming for, and how to track progress toward the target, you need a plan. A plan involves having a clear picture of your target and the actual metrics (numbers, baby!) to track your progress (or *prog-mess*, as Ted suggests).

Penalty Kick: While we clearly feel that Ted was an impressive leader, we have to call him out on this one. *"My plan is for my plan to work."* Um, Ted... that is *not* a plan.

Roy's self-improvement arc involved several different tactics, but one of the easiest to track would be the goal of cussing less in front of his niece Phoebe.

Roy shouldn't expect perfection on day one. He could ask Phoebe to track him for one week. As she racked up the pounds (money, for our non-UK friends) he owed her, at the end of the week, Roy could set a goal for the following week. He could continue this until he reached his goal of "no f*cks given."

In the business world, we keep score through KPIs,[14] which stands for key performance indicators. These KPIs help individuals or departments track their progress and contribution to the larger company vision and SMART goals. Outside of business, we might do this with badges, closed fitness circles on our smartwatches, personal development apps, smiley face stickers, graded papers, and dashboards.

Roy might have a scorecard indicating how many times he cussed in front of Phoebe, with a goal of reducing the number of "f*cks" given by 25 percent each week.

Let's take another look at Ted's SMART goal for AFC Richmond:

"Winning the whole f'ing thing!"
(aka... winning the Premier League title)

With that in mind, he could create these KPIs to support his goal:

Points Accumulated: Tracking the number of points the team earns each match (via win and draw [tie]) throughout the season is a fundamental KPI. AFC Richmond would need to consistently accumulate points to have a chance at winning the title.

Goals Scored and Conceded: Keeping track of the number of goals the team scores and the number they concede can indicate the team's offensive and defensive strengths and weaknesses.

Position in the League Table (Standings): This is a very direct measure of progress. Ted would want the team to consistently climb the league table as the season progresses.

Player Performance Metrics: Ted and his coaching staff would track individual player statistics, such as goals, assists, passes

---

[14] There are different flavors of business models. Some use KPIs (key performance indicators). Some track OKRs (objectives and key results). Others simply call them goals and target metrics. Same but different. The main point is that you must set a measurable goal so you know when you reach it.

completed, and defensive contribution, to ensure that players are contributing to the team's success.

Fan Engagement and Support: Ted places a strong emphasis on fan engagement and team spirit. Measuring attendance, fan engagement on social media, merchandise sales, and number of pints served by Mae on match day could be used to gauge the support and enthusiasm of the fanbase.

Team Morale and Unity: Ted believes in building a positive team culture. Regular team morale surveys, assessments, and feedback from Dr. Sharon Fieldstone could provide insights into the psychological wellbeing of the squad.

And if he is feeling cheeky (and you know he is), he might even add some of these):

Annual Higgins Christmas Party Attendance: The number of players attending the Higgins soiree is an indicator of how much the team enjoys spending time together, denoting team unity.

Time Out: IOHO, Season 2, Episode 4 "Carol of the Bells" is quite possibly the best Christmas sitcom episode ever produced.

Led Tasso Appearances: When Nate asks, "Who's Led Tasso?" Coach Beard replies, "The last resort." As Ted's alter ego, Led Tasso, only makes an appearance when all other options have failed to get through to the team, for this KPI, Ted would want to ensure that the number is very, very low!

Here are some other possible KPIs around AFC Richmond's cohort:

Keeley	Number of new followers of Keeley's PR firm
Rebecca	Number of tickets sold
Mae	Beverage sales on match day
The team	Pass completion rate Total percentage of match possession

We could write an entire book just on business KPIs. When our kids were teens, they probably would have liked to see KPIs around reducing the amount of nagging that went on at our houses. As for Rebecca, when she wasn't searching the internet for Rupert's latest mischief, the Richmond KPIs she had on her computer no doubt involved a great deal of financial tracking.

True confession time... We are bigger nerds than you might have suspected, and at **LeadItLikeLasso.com** we have drafted a full business plan and budget for AFC Richmond. And we may or may not have tracked the leadership qualities of the characters across each episode so you can see a visual of their arc. (You are welcome.)

Whether on the pitch, in the board room, or in our personal pursuits, success is guided by these KPIs or other measurable metrics.

Metrics are the half-time of life. Nope, that's not really right. Metrics are the *scorecard...* yes, that's better.

Having a regular cadence to review those metrics and taking the time to make adjustments is like half-time. The beautiful thing is that you get to control the clock and call as many time-outs to review as needed.

LEGACY AND SUCCESSION PLANNING

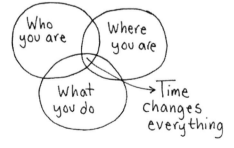

For the majority of us, we do not have to review, rehash, or relive our scores, stats, and metrics... or the actions that got us there... while sitting in a press room in front of the world.

Some of us do have to stand at the front of board rooms, classrooms, or our own living rooms and look into the eyes of the folks to whom we feel responsible.

All of us stand in front of a mirror and have to hold ourselves accountable.

We are going to hit you with a hard truth here ("Oklahoma"). The *Ted Lasso* series has come to an end. It has made us think about what legacy Ted Lasso has left behind and what he has left for the future of AFC Richmond.

He has laid the foundation for someone to continue *The ~~Lasso~~ Richmond Way*. (If you want to get lost in the internet, you can spend a day reading so many ideas of what folks hope will happen in a Season 4! Or a spin-off! Or a reunion show!)

If anyone asks us about Season 4, Marnie will be entering her cookies in the Kansas City Junior Soccer Club bake-off competition against Ted's biscuits. And Nick will be called on by Coach Roy Kent in a football press conference where he "mustache" him a question.

Our daydreams aside, the original characters of the show really did complete their story arcs. So we ask... has Ted indeed left a legacy behind? Some points to consider:

◊ Did he instill a culture that will live beyond his tenure?

◊ Did he mentor the next generation of leaders on how to carry the torch?

◊ Do they believe in the vision of a team that bonds beyond the locker room and inspires the community?

As a television show, *Ted Lasso* has certainly left a legacy. It was the first Apple streaming show to have over a billion minutes watched. It inspired podcasts, self-help groups, positivity posts, and books! It has fans wanting to become the best versions of themselves as they level up to Lead It Like Lasso.

LEAD IT LIKE LASSO

There are no shortage of authors, YouTubers, and influencers who address the notions of leveling up and legacy. Jimmy Donaldson (aka Mr. Beast) is a prime example. In 2015, Mr. Beast, who originally started a YouTube following for his gaming and challenges, uploaded videos for his future self. They ranged from 6 months to 10 years into the future.

He painted a vivid vision and committed to it by time-releasing those videos. With the target in mind, he set his sights forward. In his videos, he speaks to specific metrics in terms of the number of subscribers he would have and the amount of money he would give away. Unsurprisingly, he has already far surpassed his own expectations.

With a remarkable ability to leverage influence to his over 204 million subscribers, Mr. Beast demonstrated a keen understanding of how actions today can shape a legacy for years to come. By strategically combining his passion for content creation with philanthropy, he set a powerful precedent for aspiring leaders.

An important element in thinking about legacy is succession planning. Mr. Beast does not represent traditional success planning – although he is clearly inspiring others.

Typically as we think about succession planning, we consider how a leader plans to pass along his company, organization, or even estate to others. A critical component of that is providing the training and development of those who will find themselves responsible in the future.

In looking at how to train those who will lead that charge, there are important considerations. Conveniently enough, they fall into the lather, rinse, repeat strategy... meaning, if you create a strong culture, build a vision (with both strategic and tactical plans), and then communicate those perpetually, you will find a lot of the work is done.

The details will lie in the specific development of each of the players (i.e., future leaders).

Consider once again the coaching staff that Ted built. What seminars, team-building activities, leadership programs, mentoring, coaching, or certification courses might Roy, Coach Beard, and maybe Nate (as he works his way back up from assistant-to-the-kit man) need.

Extra Time! Developing people at all levels makes for a stronger organization and helps those within it level up. Two real-world examples (both from American football) who are often lauded for such efforts are Nick Saban, University of Alabama coach, and Andy Reid, NFL coach of the Kansas City Chiefs. Looking around top college football programs, you can find impressive head coaches who started as assistant coaches under Nick Saban. The same holds true for several NFL head coaches whose earlier careers were under Andy Reid.

If you are playing along at home, you should feel good about suiting up for the game.

Previously in *Ted Lasso* and The Training, we've seen:

◊ **Core Values & Culture**: Create a team powered by positivity

◊ **Vision & Purpose**: Help each player become the best version of themselves, which drives the team to success

◊ **Communication & Influence**: Create an entire community in support of that vision

◊ **Adaptability & Resilience**: Roll with the punches, panic attacks, and setbacks

◊ **Networks & Community**: Meet others who support and challenge you to become better

◊ **Legacy & Leveling Up**: Learn not only how to lead well but how to leave well.

We are ready. It's time to play The Game!

Interested in more readings on Legacy and Leveling Up?
Check out what might be on Beard's bookshelf...

- *Be Your Future Self Now*, Dr. Benjamin Hardy

- *10x Is Easier Than 2x*, Dan Sullivan and Dr. Benjamin Hardy

- *The Mountain Is You*, Brianna Wiest

- *Talentpreneurship*, Sunny Kaila

- *Reality is Broken*, Jane McGonigal

PART FOUR

THE GAME

10 THE GAME

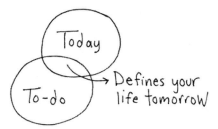

Okay. It's game time! IRL. Yeah... in real life. In *your* real life.

Say a friend stopped you on the street and asked you how things were going. You respond with "fine." We hope your friend would go all Roy Kent on you and yell, *"Fine?* Don't you dare settle for fine!"

So now that we are in The Game, we want you to paint the picture of the best version of you that you can be, and let's define the operating system to make it happen!

One of the many books in our library is *Be Your Future Self Now* by Dr. Benjamin Hardy. It very much aligns with how we look at the lessons learned from *Ted Lasso*. Dr. Hardy's philosophy is that if you can create a clear vision for the person you want to be, or the company you want to build, you will be able to drive the strategies, actions, and habits to get you there.

We suspect you are not dreaming of a future where things are only *fine*. Picture the *best* version of you, because that is what we are working toward.

Now is the time to become that person! How do you want to write your future? Will you take notes right in this book, download the forms at **LeadItLikeLasso.com**, or pull out a brand-new notebook? (We love a new notebook. It smells like potential.) Whatever it may be for you, let's go!

YOUR CORE VALUES

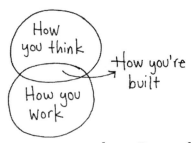

First up is to define your core values. Remember core values are fundamental principles that guide behavior, actions, and decisions (for you and/or your organization). They represent the deeply held beliefs that shape your character or your company culture. Core values serve as a compass, providing a clear sense of direction and a framework for making choices in various situations.

We are going to focus on personal core values, but this is important for organizations to do as well.

Think about moments in your life when you felt most fulfilled, proud, or aligned with your true self. Consider both personal and professional experiences. Write down the key themes, emotions, and values associated with these experiences. For example, if you felt most fulfilled when helping others, *compassion* may be one of your core values.

This might be what Ted's list looks like:

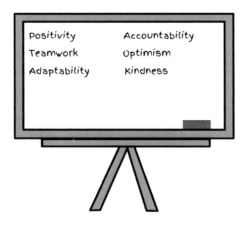

This is a timed drill so put yourself on the clock for two minutes and see how many you can come up with. If you get stuck defeating the blank page, take a look at the list below and circle the ones that resonate.

Integrity	Quality	Equality
Accountability	Kindness	Generosity
Empathy	Empowerment	Humor
Innovation	Responsibility	Consistency
Respect	Patience	Compassion
Sustainability	Creativity	Determination
Excellence	Authenticity	Optimism
Adaptability	Loyalty	Learning
Teamwork	Justice	Perseverance
Honesty	Open-mindedness	Pioneering
Diversity	Positivity	Altruism
Service	Flexibility	Purposefulness
Transparency	Independence	Ambition
Courage	Kindness	Innovation
Humility	Resilience	Harmony
Trust	Fairness	Curiosity
Gratitude	Collaboration	Authenticity
Leadership	Growth	Simplicity

Let's face it, nothing on that list sounds bad, but you can't pick them all. Consider how you consistently behave, and then prune your list to 3-6 values. Feel free to check with your Diamond Dogs to see if they agree.

You can always revise your core values later, but go ahead and jot them down now.

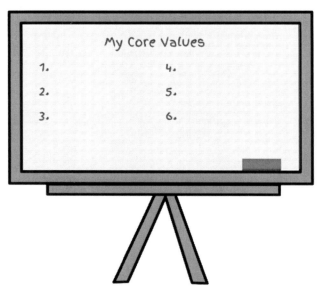

If you have a company or work for a company that has already defined its core values, see how yours compare. They do not need to be identical, but if you feel a constant clash at work, look to see if this discrepancy might be a reason.

Here are some core values that might not feel aligned.

◊ **Independence vs. Teamwork**: Independence values self-reliance and individual decision-making. It may clash with Teamwork, which emphasizes collaboration and collective decision-making.

◊ **Innovation vs. Tradition**: Innovation values new ideas, technologies, and methods. It may clash with Tradition, which cherishes established customs, practices, and beliefs.

◊ **Transparency vs. Discretion**: Transparency values open communication and sharing information. It may clash with Discretion, which values privacy and careful handling of sensitive information.

◊ **Competitiveness vs. Cooperation**: Competitiveness values striving for excellence and outperforming others. It may clash with Cooperation, which emphasizes working together harmoniously for mutual benefit.

◊ **Risk-taking vs. Caution**: Risk-taking values bold decision-making and a willingness to venture into the unknown. It may clash with Caution, which values careful consideration and minimizing potential pitfalls.

◊ **Empathy vs. Objectivity**: Empathy values understanding and considering others' feelings and perspectives. It may clash with Objectivity, which emphasizes making decisions based solely on facts and logic.

Remember, it's not that one set of values is inherently better than the other, but rather that understanding how they may conflict can help manage and navigate complex situations. In practice, finding a balance or prioritizing certain values for specific contexts is often key.

We have all heard the phrase *opposites attract*. There are characteristics and traits that can help balance each other. Though sometimes, they just cause sparks – like differing politics at the holiday dinner table.

The question to ask yourself is: When you run into misalignment, what are you going to do about it?

Think about the mismatch in core values when Keeley first started her PR firm and was working with Barbara, her Chief Financial Officer. They both had to make compromises along the way. In the end, they teamed up as partners for a new PR firm. (Should a spin-off ever happen, we would love to see the core values that help KBPR dominate the marketing world!)

Trick Play: If you are a parent, think about the core values of your children. If one has a strong "righteous sense of justice," then if you need them to do a favor, you might take the approach of balance. *"If you would do this for me, then I will do this for you…"* or *"Since your brother is going to do this chore, will you please do xyz?"*

So, we are curious (and not judgmental). Did you come up with a single core value that inspires you to hang it up on the wall at work (and maybe in your bathroom next to Ted's "Believe" sign that he looks at while justifying not flossing)? If you did, take a picture and tag us **#leaditlikelasso** and **#corevalues** so we can all see!

YOUR PERSONAL OPERATING SYSTEM

Core values absolutely are a critical part of defining your personal operating system. We believe it would be nice if we had quick access to all of our team members' operating manuals or playbooks.

Think of someone you know really well... a family member, a friend, or a colleague.

Now think about how to push their buttons (and you definitely know what they are 😊).

Remember back to Season 1, Episode 3, when Keeley told Roy she knew how to push his buttons? Of course, he disagreed. But then she started mocking him by copycatting every word that came out of his mouth. It unglued him... first, because she did it, and second, because she knew it would work.

When you know what buttons to push to make someone mad, or what to say to cheer them up or inspire them to do better, you have insights into their operating system. (FWIW, we think that resumes and profiles on job boards would be a lot more effective in finding good candidates if they included core values and other critical elements of a person's operating system.)

Many leadership programs offer personality trait assessments. They are similar to our assessment about which Lasso character you are most like. Personality assessments aim to determine how to categorize you in terms of whether you are extroverted or introverted, detail-oriented or visionary, creative or realistic... If you have done any of those, then you might be able to quickly fill out your personal operating system. Here are some questions to ask yourself to start:

_____'s Operating System
(Your name here)

Philosophy statement	What makes you tick? What are your core values that drive who you want to be and what you want to do?
Motivation	What are your love languages? What puts a fire in your belly?
De-motivation	What drags you down? What halts progress? What causes anxiety?
Personality	What are some of your strengths? Weaknesses?
Favorites	How do you de-stress? Hobbies? Core activities?
Books/Quotes/Songs	What books/quotes or songs speak to you?

We showed you what we pictured Ted's operating system to look like. Here is a glimpse of Marnie's. (Of course for the sake of Ted Lasso, we have added how we align to the Richmond Way.)

We would love to see yours! Head over to **LeadItLikeLasso.com** and fill it out with answers to your questions (and check out the operating systems for Roy, Nate, Rebecca, Jamie, Keeley, and Sam).

MARNIE STOCKMAN

- Gen X
- Author, start up founder
- "When our clients succeed, we succeed"

PHILOSOPHY

I aim to be positive and enthusiastic, bringing energy and passion to the space. I am one of those irritatingly chipper early risers who checks email at 5:15 am. I cherish my morning hours of peace before the day begins so I can do thinking work and enjoy breakfast and tea with my husband before he goes to work. I will not bother you before 8 am. I have excessively high expectations when it comes to customer success - particularly in terms of communication. Lifecycle Insights is known for being responsive. Side note: that does not mean the customer is always right.

MOTIVATION

I was a teacher and still am at heart. I take feedback well and offer it freely. If there is something I can do to help, please ask or let me know. I work fast and furious to advocate for what you need. I want to do what it takes for you to be successful.

DE-MOTIVATION

Drama, stale work, Bullies

LEADERSHIP POSITIONS

- Co-founder, CEO
- Mother
- Advisor

PERSONALITY

Patience

Analytical

Problem Solving

Handles Pressure

RICHMOND WAY

★★★★★ Belief

★★★★★ Conditioning

★★★★☆ Versatility

★★★★★ Awareness

FAVORITES/ CORE

LIBRARY

Think again, Adam Grant
Mindset, Carol, Dweck
Tipping point, Malcolm Gladwell

Isn't this more interesting than a resume? (But if you prefer that other sort of thing, go connect with MarnieStockman on LinkedIn and you can compare.)

Second, this should not just be a one-and-done document. Unlike resumes which we only dust off if we absolutely must, this document is good to review regularly. Set a reminder on your calendar every six months and see if new motivators, quotes, or aspirations resonate. Check in with how your core values are aligning at work and with those around you.

Extra Time: If you are serious about your core values, then you need to involve the whole team. Share with your team at work or with your family at the dinner table (or living room).

or...

For bonus points, create a core values list for another family member. Marnie's daughter created the first draft of hers – which led to great conversations.

YOUR COMMUNICATION GUIDE

Much like our company hot seat icebreaker activity, the personal operating system document gives a quick glimpse into your personal characteristics. (Ted would find these tidbits "lovely.") The second part of how you operate should focus on how best to communicate.

In Chapter Six, we talked about the skills and abilities a person needs to effectively communicate. We also discussed the importance of communication in terms of seeing your vision come to light. It is through communication that team members collaborate and cooperate on common goals, tasks, and tactics. This is why it is important to understand how best to work with others and how others can work with you.

There are two key elements to consider. The first is your own communication style. The second is your broader communication strategy and cadence.

Your style might include points like:

- Don't talk to me before 9 AM and coffee.
- Text first. Call second.
- I only check email twice a day.
- Please send messages by carrier pigeon.

Your broader communication plan will be more context/role specific:

- We will have 30-minute one-on-ones weekly where we will share…
- We will have department meetings on Mondays to discuss…
- We will have quarterly business reviews (QBRs) to review progress on our KPIs and SMART goals
- We will have family game night after our family meeting on Fridays (and all snow days!)

Like we said, communication plans vary by context. If you are ready to build yours, jump right in. If you need some inspiration, check out Marnie's. Or try out our game – heck, even if you don't need inspiration, play our little game. We get a lot of laughs when we hear the answers.

COMMUNICATION GUIDE

CONDITIONS I LIKE TO WORK IN

I love working remotely. I like a clean desk and new notebook. I start my day with a walk and reviewing my plan that I made sure to create before I went to bed. I like to plan ahead and organize my work - which oddly enough allows me to be more flexible if something comes up. I love working creatively to solve problems.
While I prefer working from home, I can be found working nearly anywhere.
I am a checklist girl and appreciate the accountability of to do lists (and strategic planning is just an extension of this. I like to plan my work and work my plan)

TIME/HOURS I LIKE TO WORK

BEST WAYS TO COMMUNICATE WITH ME

- During work hours, I like the first line of communication to be through Google chat. Unless you are on a call or some other event, I will expect a near immediate response as though I popped into your cubby if we were in an office. You can expect the same in return.
- If I am on a call and you need an immediate response, send a text message.
- If you want to hop on a call, just ask. If you want to schedule time for a project or something with a client, if my calendar is open, feel free to just book it.
- Email is best for any topic that will need to be referenced later. I am a zero inbox girl so I will reply

GIVING AND RECEIVING FEEDBACK

I was a teacher and still am at heart. I take feedback well and offer it freely. If there is something I can do to help, please ask or let me know. I work fast and furious so advocate for what you need. I want to do what it takes for you to be successfull
Any concern or issue should be discussed on a call. Texts and chats are tone deaf so if you think there is a problem or issue, we will talk about it not text about it.
Have a clever new idea? Share! A rising tide lifts all ships.

THINGS I NEED

I love brainstorming with others to solve problems. I need some solo time to best digest and stew on issues. I need short breaks to grab healthy snacks throughout the day. I appreciate positive energy. I need my thinking time in the morning to charge my batteries for the day.

It might seem intimidating to create a communication plan from scratch. Feel free to steal ours. Or... if you are up for a quick game, we found this to be a fun way to defeat the blank page.

Step 1: Fill in the table below. (Think MadLibs or fill-in-the-blank.)

Favorite Nickname	
Adjective	
Noun	
Noun	
Number between 1 and 10	
Number between 11 and 20	
Time period	
Time	
Mode of communication	
Adverb	
Adverb	
Noun	
Adjective	
Personal adjective	
Negative adjective	

Now use your answers to fill in the blanks in order.

Communication Guide for _____ (favorite nickname)

Conditions I like to work in:

- I like a _____ (adjective) working environment.
- I like to have my own _____(noun).
- I find it hard to work in _____(noun).

The times/hours I like to work:

- I prefer my work hours to be _____(#) to _____(#).
- I work best in the _____(time of day).
- It is best if you contact me at _____(time).

The best ways to communicate with me:

- It is best to try to reach me by_____(mode of communication).
- I read my emails _____(adverb).

The ways I like to receive feedback:

- I like to receive feedback _____(adverb).

Along with criticism, please also provide _____ (noun).

Things I need:

- Brainstorming sessions are important. I believe they need to be _____(adjective).
- I am very_____ (positive adjective), so I work hard to avoid _____ (negative adjective).

Once you stop laughing at your clearly defeated blank page (Well done! You crushed it!), you can go fill in the blanks with your real answers. (FYI having something to review or revise kicks in the critiquing part of your brain, which can complement your creative part so just throwing something out there – even a silly something – is helpful!)

Penalty kick: Many leaders state that they have an open-door policy. On the surface that sounds ideal, but what we have also found in working for lots of leaders is that open-door policies do not always translate into open communication.

In *Think Again*, Adam Grant tells a story of Melinda Gates hoping to get honest feedback from her team. Because of Melinda Gates' status and position in the company, it was not easy for her employees to disagree or challenge her ideas. Her team suggested an activity similar to "mean tweets" (where celebrities read mean tweets about themselves live and respond). In this case, people were asked to write anonymous feedback about what she could do to improve. She did the activity and as she read some of the comments, she admitted that she struggled with various situations or traits and that she would work on that. She also asked for help from her team to call her out when they saw her struggling. That vulnerability certainly led to a more effective open-door policy and better communication.

If you are a manager or team leader, you should develop a communication guide for internal and external stakeholders of your company. In-person, fully remote, and hybrid organizations all have different communication challenges, but defining your rules around communication helps everyone get on the same page, pitch, or playground.

YOUR VISION

It's now time to get moving toward your vision. We have talked a lot about what you are aiming for, so let's get down to the nitty gritty.

Part of our big vision involves seeing this book on the shelves in airports and bookstores! We are thinking big. So we want you to think big, too!

Remember, in this activity we are looking at the big picture – several years out. What are you aiming for? What does success look like? Document it.

If you are struggling, ask yourself a few more questions:

- Are you striving to hit a financial target?
- Do you have an academic goal?
- Is this a goal involving health or wellness?
- Are you aiming for a work accomplishment?
- Do you have a family goal? Or are you helping family with a goal?

You can (and you should!) come back to your vision regularly so start by putting something out there!

My vision is to: _____

Now ask yourself why you want to do this. What fuels your fire everyday? This is what you need to answer in order to define your purpose or your why.

My purpose (my why!) is: _____

Need some inspiration? Check out these examples...

Who	Vision	Purpose
Parent	To help each of my children reach their fullest potential	To provide unwavering love, support, and safety to help my children positively impact the world.
Student	To get into the college of my dreams so I can get a job and expand my world	To experience new things with friends through travel
Coach	To build winning teams who understand that winning is built through character, resilience, and teamwork	To mentor athletes toward personal growth through a culture of discipline, sportsmanship, and self-belief
Business owner	To create an innovative company that delivers exceptional value to customers and employees	To lead with integrity and foster a culture of continuous improvement through creativity and innovation
Non-profit leader	To impact society positively by mobilizing resources and fostering collaboration	To advocate for positive change and build strategic partnerships to uplift the underserved

We really want to be clear on this vision, so it's time to make it a SMART goal. Remember SMART stands for:

Specific

Measurable

Attainable

Realistic

Timebound

In _____(time period), I/we will

have _____(earned, lost, gained,

written, helped...) _____

(number of people) do_____

(big bold goal).

Here's how this fill-in-the-blank statement translates for various folks (leaders or those leveling up as leaders in their own lives).

Who	SMART Goal
Parent	For the next 3 months, I will have spent 2 hours each week of quality time with each child, tracked in a journal, helping them share their goals, dreams, and concerns while having fun.
Student	I will earn a GPA of 3.8 or above in the upcoming semester and study 30 minutes a day for my college placement exams.
Coach	In the upcoming season, we will increase our passing completion rate by 15%.
Business owner	Within the next fiscal year, we will increase our annual revenue by 20% by expanding into a new market.
Non-profit leader	In the next year, we will provide essential services to 10% more individuals in need.

Now that we have talked the talk about vision, purpose, and goals, we will walk the walk. So here's ours – IRL!

Our Vision: Write books and software to educate, entertain, and support people as they become the best version of themselves that they can be.

Our Purpose (why): We want to help people level up to a better life. We can all be better together.

SMART Goal: In 3 years, we will have sold a million copies of *Lead It Like Lasso* and have helped over 100,000 people on their journey to leveling up with our online content, platform, and challenges/quests.

Now that you have documented what you are aiming for, it's time to list your stakeholders. If you are working on a business goal, you will need to consider your employees, customers, suppliers, and press (social media, newspapers, magazines, TV). If you are working on a personal goal, you might want to consider family, peers, mentors, a coach, your employer, or community.

List the types of stakeholders you need to consider and be specific about who they are. Let's take our college student as an example. They might list the following stakeholder groups:

- Employer
- Peers
- Mentor
- Family
- Community

This is the fun part (although we've been having fun all along!). For each stakeholder, write down 2-4 quotes about the *amazing* things they will say about you/your company in 3 years when you have achieved your goal. (This is not the time to be shy or mumble your words. This is a critical step in manifesting your dreams and making it happen.)

This is what one student we work with came up with:

Stakeholder	Raving review 3 years from now
Employer	"I wish I could hire 10 more like her!"
Peers	"Wow! She is really doing well for herself."
Mentor	"Follow this human! She is going places!"
Family	"I am proud of her."
Community	"What a great person to have around!"

What would you want your stakeholders to say about you when you are a success?

We have mentioned Impostor Syndrome a couple times. Impostor Syndrome is a feeling of doubt, or the fear of being exposed as a fraud, despite already being competent or successful. If you are feeling anxious about writing amazing things down about yourself for the future, you might be letting Impostor Syndrome sneak up on you. We know it isn't easy, so we will give it a whirl and be a bit vulnerable.

Here is what we hope our readers say in reviews on Amazon:

- "Oh my gosh, I laughed from the opening line and learned from there on out."

- "F-ing amazing!"

- "Made me think! Made me smile! Reminded me a lot of the fun and feelings I had when watching *Ted Lasso*. Thanks for writing this book!"

- "I am writing my personal operating system tonight and sharing at work tomorrow!"

(Would you help us reach our vision? If you have enjoyed this book, please leave us a 5-star review on Amazon or Goodreads and also connect with us on social to share your vision. Maybe we can help with yours!)

Once you have written down those quotes, go check back up on your vision and goal statements. Do they align? Oftentimes writing such quotes provides detail and clarity that was missed when drafting a vision statement.

Now that you have an even better picture of where you are heading, let's see how you are going to make sure it happens.

The only way to get from here to there is to "plan the work and work the plan." And the one way to make sure the plan is working is by tracking your progress.

We discussed earlier that your vision and purpose work like bumper pads in bowling. They help shape the behaviors and actions to keep them funneling back to your target. The more clarity you can provide by defining your vision and purpose, the narrower your lane will be, which will dramatically improve your score.

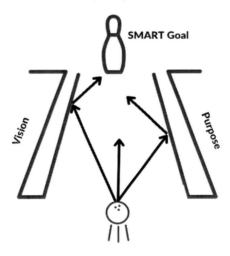

So let's get down to keeping score for ourselves.

YOUR NUMBERS

Whether you are trying to beat Rupert Mannion at darts, lose 15 pounds, or hit $2M in revenue, you must know your numbers in order to keep score.

Like we saw earlier, there are lots of ways you can use numbers to help you get to your ultimate destination. The amazing and scary thing about numbers is that they are awfully convenient for holding someone accountable.

Accountability matters... right, Keeley? *Abso-f*ckin-lutely.*

Our favorite *Ted Lasso* characters realized so much personal growth over 3 seasons. We actually built a spreadsheet to track their progress based on the leadership qualities of John Wooden's "Pyramid of Success."

Time out: While numbers don't lie, we are more than happy to admit that we might be wrong. If you want to check out the full data and provide feedback, hop on over to **LeadItLikeLasso.com** and let us know what you think. We welcome all comments, questions, complaints, and criticisms. (But we definitely prefer them to be curious rather than judgmental. ☺)

By our calculations, on a scale of 1-100, Rebecca started out at a 55.0. She dropped quickly to a 43.9. Then she eeked her way up to a 66.7 by Season 1, Episode 7. (That was the one where Keeley and Sassy worked to "Make Rebecca Great Again.") By the end of Season 3, Rebecca reached her highest level at 92.4. Sure, Rupert's shenanigans made her dip every now and then, but she made a remarkable transformation.

As we tracked her transformation, it would make a decent model for any business. Yet some businesses have growth that looks more like Roy. *"He's here, he's there. He's... (yeah...) every f*cking where."* Most important for Roy though, was that despite some backsliding, he definitely aimed to improve, made many gains, and still wanted to continue to grow.

There are clearly lots of paths to help you reach your goal. The first step you need to take is to write down 3 numbers:

1. What is your starting number?
2. What is your goal number?

3. How long will it take you to get from 1-2?

Marnie was a math teacher so she literally could go on for days, but don't worry because Nick is going to keep her in check.

Think about the path you want to take. We will give you two options: slow and steady, or hockey stick.

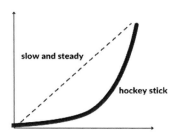

If you are aiming to lose weight, slow and steady is the way to go. If you are scaling a Software-as-a-Service (SaaS) business, hockey stick growth is the goal.

Fill in the boxes below to help set your targets.

NOTE: This is built for a 3-year goal. If you have a different timeframe, modify the chart.

DO THE MATH…

Slow and steady:
Subtract your *Starting spot* from your *End goal*.
Divide that number by 3 to get your *Yearly increase*.
Add *Yearly increase* to your *Starting spot* to get *Year 1*.
Add *Yearly increase* to *Year 1* to get *Year 2*.
If you like to check your work (and we would like that), add *Yearly increase* to *Year 2* and make sure you land at your *End goal*.

Hockey stick:
Subtract your *Starting spot* from your *End goal* to get the *difference*.
Take your *difference* and divide by 2.
Subtract that *difference* from your *End Goal* and put it in the *Year 2* box.
Divide the *difference* by 2 (feel free to round!) and subtract that from *Year 2* to get *Year 1*.

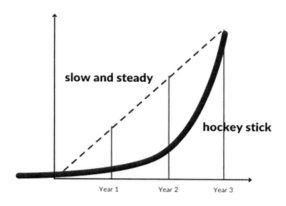

	Starting	Year 1	Year 2	End goal
Slow & steady				
Hockey stick				

Now that you have annual goals, you have to keep going, otherwise this activity will turn into a failed New Year's Resolution. Yeah, we know what happens with most of those.

Take your annual goals and break them into quarterly objectives. Use those quarterly goals to create monthly outcomes. And from those, create your weekly task list and your daily to dos! That is how you will get things done!

	Starting	Year 1	Year 2	End goal
Slow & steady	$500	$3667	$6833	$10,000
Hockey stick	$500	$2875	$5250	$10,000

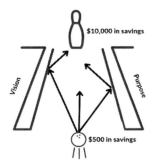

The student who built this chart decided to aim for the hockey stick growth because of their graduation and expectation to make more money each year. So for Year 1, the goal was to save an additional $2375. This meant they needed to save $200 a month, which is approximately $50 per week, or about $7 a day. When looked at this way, it helped make simple decisions about reducing splurge foods and drinks, plus being conscious of not wasting extra gas driving around unnecessarily. It helped the savings target feel completely doable. This student is well on their way to the goal.

YOUR DIAMOND DOGS

Ted's closest connections as a coach were clearly the Diamond Dogs. They were a critical component to his mental wellbeing and success. When we talked about developing a support network, this is a shining example.

Time out: Sometimes "support network" is a misnomer. We prefer "challenge network."

The Diamond Dogs did not form so they could blindly go along with what someone asked. (Heck, Coach Beard and Nate gave Ted the silent treatment until he agreed to talk to Roy about benching him.) They were honest, open, and vulnerable with each other. They were willing to call each other out. They challenged each other to be better.

It is said that you are the average of your five closest connections, and John Wooden says you will never outperform your inner circle. Who are your closest five connections? Take a minute to write them down.

1.

2.

3.

4.

5.

Now look at your list. Are these 5 people truly members of your challenge network? Do they make you better?

If you struggle answering that, the 5 Whys activity is a great way to help you work through it.

Ted would undoubtedly list Coach Beard at the top of his Diamond Dogs because Beard makes Ted better...

1. **Why** is Ted friends with Coach Beard?
   Because they have a shared passion for football and coaching.

2. **Why** does their shared passion for football and coaching make them friends?
   Because it provides them with a common purpose and a deep understanding of each other's work.

3. **Why** does having a common purpose and understanding of each other's work make them friends?
   Because it creates a strong foundation for mutual respect and trust.

4. **Why** does mutual respect and trust form the basis of their friendship?

MARNIE STOCKMAN AND NICK CONIGLIO

Because it allows them to have open, honest, and meaningful conversations about their goals and challenges.

5. **Why** do open, honest, and meaningful conversations about their goals and challenges strengthen their friendship?
Because it enables Coach Beard to offer valuable insights, support, and guidance that ultimately make Ted a better coach and person.

So, Coach Beard makes Ted a better person because he provides a foundation of mutual respect and trust, allowing for open and meaningful conversations that result in valuable insights and support for Ted's growth and development as a coach and human being. This dynamic strengthens their friendship and enhances Ted's overall effectiveness.

That is a pretty compelling argument for why Coach Beard heads up the Diamond Dogs for Ted. How is your list looking?

It's important to reflect. It is even more important to see how you are showing up for others for whom you are their Diamond Dog. If they asked the 5 Whys of you, what would the answers look like?

Once you have decided who your 5 people are, enter their initials in the table on the next page. Then put an *x* in any box where that person truly supports and/or challenges you. Notice any patterns? Missing any areas?

	DD 1	DD 2	DD 3	DD 4	DD 5
name ___	___	___	___	___	___
Physical					
Social					
Emotional					
Mental health					
Spiritual					
Intellectual					

The first time we did this activity with a group of students, we found a common trend. Their Diamond Dogs all checked the social boxes and maybe one other. They didn't, however, fully support the student.

It is interesting to note that many years later, when we caught up with those students, the most successful of them had formed a more supportive and well-rounded group of Diamond Dogs. While some of their former Diamond Dogs have indeed been "relegated" out of their inner circle, many are still friends. They just don't hold the same influence. So, you must ask yourself the tough questions: Does each member of your Diamond Dogs make you better? Is there a specific area where you know you need more support? Where can you find a human to support you in that area?

Let us be clear. That is a very easy question to ask. But for some, it might not be an easy question to answer. If you are just starting to build your network, or you are unsure of how to find your Diamond Dogs, we remind you that there is work to do. In the next section, we will share lots of networking ideas on how to get started. Remember that it is your core values and vision that drive you, so you want to look for support in those areas.

> **Time out**: If you are a Harry Potter fan in addition to being a raving Lasso fan, then you might recall that Neville earned the winning point for Gryffindor... by standing up to his friends when he thought their behavior was wrong. That is the kind of respect a true Diamond Dog would lend.

We have certainly seen many folks who have Diamond Dogs in their personal lives, but it is more of a challenge for them to find that same level of support in their professional lives. CEOs of companies, superintendents of school systems, and presidents of colleges often find themselves siloed off because of their leadership position (similar to Melinda Gates). That is when finding a peer group should make it to the top of your to do list.

In the business world, there are often industry-specific peer groups, sometimes referred to as mastermind groups. These are different from networking groups which we will discuss later. They are dedicated peer cohorts who commit to work together as accountability groups, sounding boards, advisory councils, peer coaches, and emotional support team members. Finding true peers to be able to have open, honest conversations about your business and the ups and downs is incredibly impactful.

One note on getting serious about peer groups and your Diamond Dogs... When done well, you *will* be held accountable. So if you are committed to making progress toward your vision, they will help you on your path. Remember those numbers we talked about. Your Diamond Dogs will expect you to show up and make progress in hitting them.

YOUR NETWORK

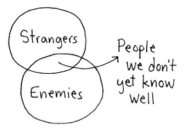

If you are like Ted Lasso, you have never met a stranger. You will take an "ussie" with a guy on a plane, play soccer with a girl on the sidewalk, and invite a street musician (busker, for our UK friends) to come play for a charity gala.

Like Ted or Keeley or Rebecca, you might already have an established network. (If that sounds like you, we hope you can still pick up a tip or two.) If you are new to networking or introverted by nature, you might be looking for some ideas and maybe a little kick in the tail.

Part of the magic of Ted Lasso was his vulnerability and authenticity. He was comfortable in his own skin and confident that the approach he was taking at AFC Richmond was the right one. He would talk and connect with anyone – even those calling him names.

Penalty Kick: Except... when Ted met Dr. Sharon Fieldstone. In the what-not-to-do category of networking, Ted had several awkward starts with Dr. Sharon. We learned later that this came from a place of distrust and fear after previous negative experiences with counseling. Once he finally learned to trust her, however, she became a rock for him to rely on. (And we dare say Ted was good for Dr. Sharon, too.)

Okay. Back to networking.

Networking is an invaluable skill in both personal and professional life. It opens doors to new opportunities, fosters meaningful relationships, and expands your knowledge base.

It is also a lot like landscaping. As they say, the best time to plant a tree was 20 years ago. The next best time is today. The same holds true for networking.

Some folks are connectors naturally and "collect" people from an early age. Who is your go-to person if you are looking for someone who might have a contact to help you with a project? That might be locating a contractor or finding a new job opportunity (or getting someone at the newspaper to pull a potentially compromising photo of Ted and Keeley ☺). Yeah, that's your connector.

If that is you, feel free to jump ahead. If it isn't, then play along to grow your network.

Traditional networking can be done formally at events, interest group meetings, conferences, or happy hours. Or it can be done informally... literally anywhere.

James Clear in *Atomic Habits* had this to say:

> "The most effective network strategy I've found has nothing to do with conferences, cocktail hours, cold emails, or any of the common ideas you hear.
>
> 1) Do interesting things.
> 2) Share them publicly.
>
> Repeat those two strategies and you'll become a magnet. Like-minded people will come to you."

Ready to start now? If you love the personal operating system document you just created, share it on social! Tag us **#leaditlikelasso** and we will happily share with our network.

This is absolutely a great way to network, but your situation might require the balance of the long game with your short-term goals. Let's take a look.

What are your networking goals? Are you looking for career opportunities, seeking mentorship, or aiming to expand your knowledge base? Jot them down now.

The next question to ask yourself is: Where do the folks who have experience, opportunities, jobs, and influence in your area of interest gather, group, or get guidance? List those places... both virtual and in-person. You will want to find ways to get involved there.

Trick play: Like, comment, and share those folks in your network. People notice people who notice them.

In any of those cases, you will want to be prepared to share a bit about yourself. If you look at research on traditional networking, you will find recommendations to write your personal elevator pitch (lasting just 60 seconds).

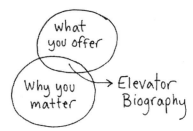

They typically look something like this.

Marketing Professional

"Hi, I'm Sarah. I'm a seasoned marketing professional with a track record of driving brand visibility and engagement. In my last role at XYZ Agency, I led a team that increased our client's online reach by 30% in just six months. I'm passionate about leveraging data-driven insights to create impactful campaigns. I'm currently exploring opportunities to apply my expertise in a dynamic and growth-focused environment."

Software Developer

"Hey, I'm Aron. I'm a full-stack developer with a passion for building user-centric applications. I've spent the last 5 years at Tech Innovators, where I led the development of our flagship product, which saw a 40% increase in user engagement. I thrive in collaborative environments and love solving complex problems. Currently, I'm seeking a role where I can contribute to innovative projects and work with a team that shares my passion for tech."

While the same type of information is covered in each, these pitches all started by naming a job. Remember, you are *not* your job. Start with your values and vision instead.

Check out Keeley's example:

"Hi! I'm Keeley Jones! I am passionate about helping companies grow their brand. I was a model and social media influencer who learned that I'd rather be a lion than a panda. I use my lioness powers to create strong brands and powerful following for the companies my PR firm represents. If you are looking to lead your company's brand to new levels, give me a shout (or a roar)."

Try it. Let's write your *Elevator Biography*.
(You still only have 60 seconds, so let's focus, baby!)

Hello/Hi/Hey, (or Howdy, if you're from the Midwest like Ted).

I am _____ (name)

I am passionate about _____

I have done this by _____.

My strength in _____ allows me to

_____ for

I am now (or now looking for) _____

Contact me if I could help you by _____.

Extra Time: We have watched hundreds of businesses give their elevator pitches. They often make the same mistake of starting with what they do (we sell flux capacitors, we have buttons that do *xyz*, we have versions in 6 different colors). Instead, they need to start with who they help and what problem they solve.

If you are writing an elevator pitch for your business, you should follow a format like this:

_____(my business)

helps _____(people it helps)

_____(solve a problem)

by _____(doing what)

After you have created an elevator biography you like, be sure to update your resume, profiles, and social media "about" sections to correspond. The more authentic you feel when others are reading your biography, the more you will attract the right network and opportunities.

YOUR LEGACY

As you contemplate your legacy, please remember that it is a personal and evolving process. It's not just about financial assets; it encompasses your core values, the impact you make on others, and the way you contribute to your community and the world.

When thinking about legacy from a leadership perspective, Simon Sinek says, "a leader's legacy is only as strong as the foundation they leave behind that allows others to continue to advance the organization in their name." Sinek continues that, "legacy is not the memory of better times when the old leader was there – that is not legacy, that's nostalgia."

Let's summarize the key points above:

◊   A legacy should provide the foundation for an organization/ family/movement so that entity can continue to advance regardless of an individual.

◊   A legacy should encompass a set of core values.

◊   A legacy will live on based on how others are impacted.

◊   A legacy can impact a broader community and even the world.

◊   An individual or company should consider their legacy to be an evolving process.

Is there any doubt that Ted left behind a legacy at AFC Richmond that would allow them to get better in the years after Ted leaves? No doubt. We are confident that if there ever was a Season 4, Roy (with the help of Nate and Beard) would take over as gaffer and continue to preach (and advance!) the core values that Ted laid out, and success would continue for AFC Richmond.

Do you believe Ted was actively thinking about his legacy during his time at AFC Richmond? Probably not. But do we believe there is any value in considering your legacy in the midst of being a leader? Absolutely!

Sure, it's true that if you have a very well-defined set of core values, a vision, effective communication, and always work to be the best version of yourself... you will, by default, create a legacy. That being said, we believe that considering your legacy early and somewhat frequently (every couple of years) can help you remain focused. As a bonus (extra time, anyone?)... Considering your legacy might also force you to think about how you can impact your broader network, community, and world. To us, that is exciting!

An advantage to projecting your legacy early is that it can act as an extra bumper pad in your journey to become the best version of yourself. Take Nate, for example. We have not spent much time profiling Nate in this book – primarily because of the jagged path his character took later in the show.

Nate started off with such promise. From a shy kit man who lacked confidence to the person who told Roy he was old and slow and needed to be angry again (like he was "angry at the grass"), Nate was on a great trajectory in his career and leadership development.

That development came to a grinding halt midway through Season 2. So much so that he became as much of a villain as Rupert. There is no other way to say it... Nate went off the rails.

As Season 3 wrapped up, Nate righted his ship a bit and began to redeem himself. For many of us, it was a slow turn... but Nate was getting there (all the way back to assistant-to-the-kit-man).

We ask this question. Imagine if Nate at the end of Season 1 had gone through the activity of trying to define what his legacy might be when he someday retired as a football coach. Do you think it would've been about dating super models, ostracizing his players and peers/coaches, or driving expensive cars? We don't think so at all. It likely would've been about finding the love of his life, having a trusted network (Nate loved the Diamond Dogs), and being respected enough to be able to reserve a table with a window-view at his favorite restaurant in Tooting.

Remember: "What is inspected is expected." Well, you can't inspect something that does not exist. Nate had never contemplated his legacy. But if he had, it could have acted as a bumper pad for him, protecting him from going off the rails. So, while not a cure-all, projecting your legacy is a tool in your toolkit to stay aligned with becoming a better you.

We know... we're in the Game section of this book so let's get playing again. Let's talk about a way to project your legacy.

It is time to choose your own adventure! The first option is to announce your own retirement in the form of an email to your company. We suggest this choice when thinking about legacy for a leader within a business or an organization.

The second choice is to write your own obituary. Morbid... we know. But boy, oh boy... does this make you think. This choice can apply to a parent, a mentor, or even a business leader. Basically anyone.

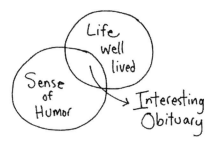

In this book, we are going to follow the activity for your retirement email. If you want to review the obituary activity, please visit **LeadItLikeLasso.com**.

Remember, you are projecting here. So where appropriate, think about the best version of your future self rather than where you are today!

Retirement Announcement Questions

When will you retire? _____

When did you start your career? _____

What was your first job title? _____

What were your initial career goals/aspirations?

_____

_____

_____

What are your projected accomplishments?

_____

_____

_____

_____

_____

What are your core values?

_____

_____

_____

_____

Identify influential colleagues, mentors, and peers.
What did you appreciate about them?

Person	What I appreciated about them

List any persons you mentored.

_____

_____

What are your post-retirement plans and/or activities?

_____

_____

How would you like to impact your community?

_____

_____

What is something fun and unique that you excel at?

_____

_____

Now for the fun part. Use the data you collected to write your retirement email! We have a template for this at **LeadItLikeLasso.com**.

Since we opened up a can of Nate the Great, let's use him as an example. For the sake of this activity, we are going to assume a spin-off has been created and Nate has become the assistant coach to Roy (the new head coach) at AFC Richmond in the year 1 A.T. (After Ted).

Nate has filled out this activity with the following responses:

NATE'S Retirement Announcement Questions

When will you retire? **30 years from now**

When did you start your career? **2018**

What was your first job title? **kit man**

What are your career goals/aspirations?

Make my dad proud

What are your projected accomplishments?

Coach AFC Richmond

Coach English National team

Win 20 trophies across all competitions

What are your core values?

positivity, fairness, empathy,

unity, unwavering support for the little guy

Name influential colleagues, mentors, and peers.
What did you appreciate about them?

Mentor	What I appreciated about them
Ted Lasso	Friend, mentor seeing my potential and never giving up
Roy Kent	Showing me how to be honest with myself and my team
Coach Beard	Gave me my first big shot and provided my one last chance in the world of football

List any persons you mentored.

Will Kitman

What are your post-retirement plans and/or activities?

Spend time with my wife Jade and our son

Honor my dad

Play the violin

How would you like to impact your community?

Give back to my community, specifically students who use skills

from athletics to advance their professional career

What is something fun and unique that you excel at?

I have a knack for creative boxes!

Responses gathered! Now let's create the retirement announcement email. Here it is (Nate-specific data is in bold)!

Nathan Shelley Retirement Announcement:
A New Chapter Begins

It is with great excitement that I announce my retirement, marking the end of a **30-year** career journey. As I look back on the milestones and experiences that have shaped my life, I am grateful for the opportunities and growth I've encountered along the way.

In **2018**, I embarked on a career in football as a **kit man** with a simple vision to **make my dad proud**. Over the years, I have had the privilege of **leading AFC Richmond and the English National Team, with our teams winning 20 trophies across all competitions**. All the while, I've learned valuable lessons that have helped me become the person I am today.

After some poor choices early in my career, I've been guided by a commitment of **positivity, fairness, empathy, unity, and an unwavering support for the little guy**, all of which have influenced most every decision I've made. I'm proud to have been part of a team that exemplified dedication, innovation, and teamwork.

As a colleague, I've been fortunate to work with incredible individuals who have inspired me and contributed to my growth. I want to share my appreciation with **Ted Lasso for being a friend, mentor, and for seeing my potential and never giving up on me.** To **Coach Beard – you were instrumental in providing both my first big shot in the world of football and providing the one last chance I had to set my path straight.** And to **Roy Kent… having you by my side for the last 28 years has been instrumental in showing me how to be honest with myself and my team**.

I have also had the pleasure of serving as a mentor to so many young coaches. To you, **Will Kitman, it has been an extraordinary pleasure to see you rise from the actual kit man to Coach Kitman.** I am pleased you will be taking over AFC Richmond and am excited to see you take the club to yet another level!

In my retirement, I'm eager to **spend more time with my beautiful wife Jade and our only son Willis**. Of course, **you can still find me playing violin in the Nelson Road Community Orchestra on the first Thursday of each month**. I am also eager to explore new horizons and am pleased to announce the **Lloyd Shelley West London Scholarship Fund in memory of my dad. This organization will provide funding for high school student athletes to pursue an education after graduating high school**.

I extend my deepest gratitude to all those who have been a part of my journey, from my colleagues and mentors to my friends and family. Your support and encouragement have been invaluable to me.

I am confident that the principles and values that guided me in my professional life will continue to be sources of inspiration, not only for me but for those I've had the privilege to work with.

As I step into this new chapter, I look forward to embracing the opportunities and challenges that retirement brings. Thank you for being a part of my journey, and I'm excited to see where the future takes me.

One more thing... **in the office lobby I have left a suggestion box (the one with grey hair on top). If any of you have any 'out of the box' ideas for me post-retirement... please drop it in the box!**

With heartfelt gratitude and best wishes,

Coach Nathan Shelley

Extra Time! Challenge yourself. Take a good hard look in the mirror. (And please don't spit at it like Nate did.) Define the legacy that would make you proud.

Check out the full Retirement
and Obituary templates online:
LeadItLikeLasso.com

CONCLUSION

While many of the ideas here might seem like common sense, we can almost hear Ted saying: *"Yeah well, common sense ain't all that common. If it was, everyone would already be living as their best selves."*

We wrote this book with the belief that leadership is life, and that we can all level up if we learn to Lead It Like Lasso.

What does it mean to Lead It Like Lasso?

It means to create and nurture an environment that helps you, your team, your company, and your friends and family to not just grow, but to evolve and flourish.

> It is positive.
> It is supportive.
> It is about relationships.
> It is about communication.
> It is about believing.
> It is about passion.
> It is about life.

People do not become leaders overnight, so we hope that as you play the Game (both here and IRL), you have outlined a path to get you heading in the right direction.

In the spirit of Ted Lasso, we encourage you to always work to become the best version of yourself. Before you set this book down to do that, poke your head into one last press conference... Lasso style.

Marnie and Nick: All right, who's next? ... Yes, Imaginary Trent, go ahead.

IT: Imaginary Trent Crimm, The Independent. You mentioned at the outset of this book that you are "relative nobodies." What authority do you have for writing a book about leadership?

Nick: Since I'm the *real* nobody here (Marnie already has 3 books published and is frequently requested to appear on podcasts and such), I will field this question.

I remember after my wife and I had our first and only child, he had some minor complications that required monitoring. We stayed in the hospital for a couple of days, only seeing him for an hour or two each day. Finally, a clean bill of health was given, and we were told we were being discharged. The only thing I remember was thinking (like every other first-time parent)... *are they really going to let us leave with this child?* We have NO idea what to do! What authority do I have to take this human being home?

So Trent, I'm not sure if we have any authority. Have we been in leadership positions? Yes. Have we seen success using the tenets outlined in this book? Absolutely. Did we make mistakes along the way? Of course. Have we tried to learn from those mistakes? Definitely – and we hope others can learn from all of that. Even more importantly, we hope others will continue the conversation to help everyone keep growing and leveling up.

Marnie: Next question? ... Um okay... Imaginary Trent, shoot!

IT: Imaginary Trent Crimm, The Independent. Is there a particular audience you are trying to reach with this book?

Marnie: Great question. Many times while writing the book, some of the topics hit close to home. We both have children who are at the age where they are trying to figure out what they want to do with their lives. We hope to reach anyone who is looking to find their path, set a goal for themselves, or create a vision bigger than their current reality.

For those currently in leadership positions, we can only hope some of these stories, strategies, and tactics will help them become better versions of themselves. And if they see people in their care who would benefit from these lessons, we hope they would help them with the Training they need to level up.

Nick: I vividly remember some times in my life like… walking into a major league baseball stadium the first time… waking up on Christmas morning when I was younger. Those are the kinds of times that we never ever want to forget, because they remind us of such joy, optimism, and wonder. It was kinda like that with this book. Like so many other people, we loved the way *Ted Lasso* made us feel. We want to keep that spirit alive and thriving as long as possible… and writing a book about Lasso gave us an excuse to give in to that feeling. For that reason, we hope this book appeals to *Ted Lasso* fanatics everywhere.

Fake Higgins: All right, we have time for one last question.

(Imaginary Trent raises his hand one last time)

Marnie: Imaginary Trent… go!

IT: Imaginary Trent Crimm, The Independent. Your book ends with a section about legacy. I'm wondering if you have any thoughts about the kind of legacy this book will leave behind?

Marnie: Oh, we have all kinds of thoughts about that. When I first began my career as a high school math teacher, students would question me about why I chose to be a teacher. As I said at the beginning of the book, it was because I believe teachers have the privilege of helping children learn, grow, and succeed on their path to becoming the best version of themselves they can be. And as we have said multiple times, what you do for a living doesn't define you as much as who you are every single day. So I would still say that I am a teacher at my core, even though I have left the school building. Thanks to the world of technology, we really are in a place where the whole world can be our classroom.

Both Nick and I have had the opportunity to work with lots of groups. I've probably tutored as many people at my kitchen table as I ever taught in a classroom. Nick has hired and led more teams than he ever anticipated back when he started coding in college. And through starting and selling a company, we've seen many things that are challenges for students, career-changers, and leaders today. We believe we can help to create some improvements using software.

We've played the Game outlined above and projected our own imaginary future Retirement Announcement. Here's an excerpt:

We are excited to be able to hand over the reins of our company to the people who have helped us build it. Together we have...

...connected with so many readers online and have brought value to as many as possible.

...been the impetus for some entertaining dinner table, water cooler, and Zoom chat conversations.

...helped people define and live their core values.

...helped folks find internships and jobs that align to those core values.

...created a platform to match folks with "the job they love to do so they never feel like they work a day in their lives."

...make it easy for people to show how their life experiences equate to strengths and skills that employers are looking for.

...connected folks to others to build strong networks and communities.

...helped people understand that leading their life and their companies means living and working authentically.

Thanks for asking, Imaginary Trent! And thanks for reading!

Onward. Forward.

Barbecue Sauce

RESOURCES

For additional activities, blogs,
and ways to connect and engage,
head to: **LeadItLikeLasso.com**

Bradberry, Travis, and Jean Greaves. *Emotional Intelligence 2.0.* Talent Smart, 2009.

Brown, Brené. *Braving the Wilderness: The Quest for True Belonging and the Courage to Stand Alone.* Random House, 2019.

Brown, Brené. *Dare to Lead: Brave Work. Tough Conversations. Whole Hearts.* Random House, 2018.

Brown, Brené. *Daring Greatly: How the Courage to Be Vulnerable Transforms the Way We Live, Love, Parent, and Lead.* Avery, 2015.

Burg, Bob, and John David Mann. *The Go Giver: A Little Story About a Powerful Business Idea.* Portfolio, 2015.

Cain, Susan. *Quiet: The Power of Introverts in a World That Can't Stop Talking.* Crown, 2013.

Clear, James. *Atomic Habits: An Easy & Proven Way to Build Good Habits & Break Bad Ones.* Avery, 2018.

Collins, Jim. *Good to Great: Why Some Companies Make the Leap and Others Don't.* Harper Business, 2001.

Coyle, Daniel. *The Culture Code: The Secrets of Highly Successful Groups.* Bantam, 2018.

Cunningham, Keith J. *The Road Less Stupid: Advice from the Chairman of the Board.* Keys to the Vault, 2017.

Edelman, Marian Wright. *The Measure of Our Success: A Letter to My Children and Yours.* Beacon Press, 1992.

Fowler, James H., and Nicholas Christakis. *Connected: The Surprising Power of Our Social Networks and How They Shape Our Lives—How Your Friends' Friends' Friends Affect Everything You Feel, Think, and Do.* Little, Brown Spark, 2009.

Gladwell, Malcolm. *Tipping Point: How Little Things Can Make a Big Difference*. Little, Brown, 2000.

Goleman, Daniel. *Emotional Intelligence: Why It Can Matter More Than IQ*. Bantam, 2006.

Gordon, Jon, and Mike Smith. *You Win in the Locker Room First: The 7 Cs to Build a Winning Team in Business, Sports, and Life*. Wiley, 2015.

Hardy, Benjamin. *Be Your Future Self Now: The Science of Intentional Transformation*. Hay House, 2022.

Jenkins, Carol, and Elizabeth Gardner Hines. *Black Titan: A.G. Gaston and the Making of a Black American Millionaire*. One World, 2003.

Kaila, Sunny. *Talentpreneurship: How to Build a Healthy Business, Transform the People Around You, and Live the Life of Your Dreams*. Ethos Collective, 2023.

Kotter, John P. *Leading Change*. Harvard Business, 2012.

Krzyzewski, Mike, with Donald T. Phillips. *Leading with the Heart: Coach K's Successful Strategies for Basketball, Business, and Life*. Warner Books, 2000.

Lencioni, Patrick. *Getting Naked: A Business Fable About Shedding the Three Fears That Sabotage Client Loyalty*. Jossey-Bass, 2010.

Martell, Dan. *Buy Back Your Time: Get Unstuck, Reclaim Your Freedom, and Build Your Empire*. Portfolio, 2023.

Maxwell, John C. *The Power of Five: For Network Marketing*. Maxwell Leadership, 2019.

McGonigal, Jane. *Reality Is Broken: Why Games Make Us Better and How They Can Change the World*. Penguin, 2011.

Murphy, Mark. *Hundred Percenters: Challenge Your Employees to Give It Their All, and They'll Give You Even More*. McGraw Hill, 2010.

Parker, Priya. *The Art of Gathering: How We Meet and Why It Matters*. Riverhead Books, 2018.

Peale, Norman Vincent. *The Power of Positive Thinking.* Vermillion, 2012.

Pink, Daniel H. *Drive: The Surprising Truth About What Motivates Us.* Riverhead Books, 2009.

Pink, Daniel H. *To Sell Is Human: The Surprising Truth About Moving Others.* Riverhead Books, 2012.

Polish, Joe. *What's In It for Them? 9 Genius Networking Principles to Get What You Want by Helping Others Get What They Want.* Hay House, 2022.

Ries, Eric. *The Lean Startup: How Today's Entrepreneurs Use Continuous Innovation to Create Radically Successful Businesses.* Crown Currency, 2011.

Scott, Kim. *Radical Candor: Be a Kick-Ass Boss Without Losing Your Humanity.* St. Martin's Press, 2017.

Sinek, Simon. *Infinite Game.* Portfolio, 2019.

Sinek, Simon. *Leaders Eat Last: Why Some Teams Pull Together and Others Don't.* Portfolio, 2014.

Sinek, Simon. *Start with Why: How Great Leaders Inspire Everyone to Take Action.* Portfolio, 2009.

Sullivan, Dan, and Dr. Benjamin Hardy. *Who Not How: The Formula to Achieve Bigger Goals Through Accelerating Teamwork.* Hay House, 2020.

Sullivan, Dan, and Dr. Benjamin Hardy. *10x Is Easier Than 2x: How World-Class Entrepreneurs Achieve More by Doing Less.* Hay House, 2023.

Wickman, Gino. *Traction: Get a Grip on Your Business.* BenBella Books, 2012.

Wiest, Brianna. *The Mountain Is You: Transforming Self-Sabotage into Self-Mastery.* Thought Catalog Books, 2020.

Willink, Jocko, and Leif Babin. *Extreme Ownership: How U.S. Navy SEALs Lead and Win.* St. Martin's Press, 2017.

Wiseman, Liz. *Multipliers: How the Best Leaders Make Everyone Smarter.* Harper Business, 2017.

ACKNOWLEDGMENTS

To *Ted Lasso* fans everywhere. We thank you for loving the show like we did. We hope you can agree that if we all lead our lives more like Lasso, the world will be a better place.

To our Diamond Dogs who are our biggest fans and harshest critics, we thank you for making us better. Keep at it! We are always aiming to level up!

To Demi Stevens, our amazing editor, who makes for a great accountabilibuddy and is an enthusiastic supporter. She is also an impressive force to be reckoned with.

To Jessica Hagy, our illustrator, who has a great sense of humor, unique perspective on life, and a most entertaining way of making graphs fun.

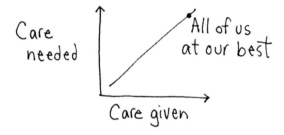

"I hope either all of us, or none of us, are judged by the actions of our weakest moments. But rather, by the strength we show when, and if, we're ever given a second chance." —Ted Lasso

With that in mind, any errors in the book are ours and ours alone.

ABOUT THE AUTHORS

Marnie Stockman, **Ed.D.**, started her career in leadership with the toughest customers/employees of all… high school math students. Her passion for education and using data and humor to help others grow and succeed took her from the classroom to Sr. Director of Customer Success of a leading Ed Tech company, and now to Co-Founder and former CEO of Lifecycle Insights – a vCIO/Customer Success platform for MSPs.

After her successful exit from Lifecycle Insights, Marnie is working on a new project as well as mentoring and advising software startups in the IT and EdTech space.

Marnie can talk to a wall, but she would rather talk to a crowd. You can often see her at IT or Ed Tech industry events. She has podcasted with many. She participates on an advisory council for CompTIA. She enjoys wrangling other leaders and SaaS founders to engage in fun and educational content to help grow businesses. She hosts the monthly Bits and Books open book club for MSP Media Network to drive conversations around leadership and business.

Her parents raised her and her sister with their own set of rules. Two of the most frequently heard ones were:

- Dad: "Don't be sorry. Be right."
- Mom: "Kill 'em with kindness."

When she isn't walking and writing books, she can be found playing pickleball or working on projects with her husband, Frank, and two 20-something kids, David and Josie, in Greensboro, Maryland.

Nick Coniglio is a seasoned technology veteran with over three decades of experience in the ever-evolving world of IT. Born with an insatiable passion for problem-solving and a gift for unraveling the mysteries behind technology's hiccups, Nick embarked on his tech odyssey in the early 1990s as a mainframe programmer.

Nick has donned numerous hats, transitioning from programmer to team lead/manager and from corporate executive to tech startup entrepreneur. His expertise spans diverse technologies and experiences, yet his greatest successes are rooted in his ability to bridge the gap between business and technology stakeholders. Nick's last two decades were marked by his leadership in four different companies, each of which experienced remarkable growth and successful exits.

Nick's most recent venture was co-founding Lifecycle Insights, which transformed from an idea into a rewarding exit in a mere three years. Following this exciting chapter, Nick is currently engaged in various projects, where he eagerly shares his wealth of experiences to lead and nurture successful teams.

Nick's problem-solving mindset carries over into his personal life. He's continually puzzled by two persistent mysteries: why his golf game hasn't improved despite playing for four decades, and the unwavering devotion and passion he holds for the New York Jets.

Nick and his wife Susan call Suwanee, Georgia, their home. When they're not busy, you'll often find them indulging in binge-watching shows like *Ted Lasso* – a shared endeavor to avoid micromanaging their nineteen-year-old son Connor, who is currently a sophomore at the University of Georgia.